KP'16

The College Student's Introduction to the Trinity

Lynne Faber Lorenzen

D0096219

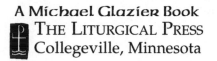

A Michael Glazier Book
THE LITURGICAL PRESS
Collegeville, Minnesota

Cover design by David Manahan, O.S.B. Illustration: Der Landgrafen Psalter, manuscript detail: *The Trinity;* 13th cent., Wurttenberg Library.

A Michael Glazier Book published by The Liturgical Press

	2	3	4	5	6	7	8

Library of Congress Cataloging-in-Publication Data

Lorenzen, Lynne Faber, 1945– .
    The college student's introduction to the Trinity / Lynne Faber
Lorenzen.
       p. cm.
    "A Michael Glazier book."
    Includes bibliographical references and index.
    ISBN 0-8146-5518-1 (alk. paper)
    1. Trinity. 2. Process theology. I. Title.
BT111.2.L67 1998
231'.044—dc21
                                              98–25617
                                                 CIP

For my family:
Parents: Jesse and Gwen Faber
Spouse: Robert Lorenzen and
Children: Janet and Mark Lorenzen

Contents

Introduction

In Western Christianity at the present time the doctrine of the Trinity is truly an enigma. On the one hand this doctrine is the foundation of liturgical worship including the greeting, "The grace of our Lord Jesus Christ, the love of God, and the communion of the Holy Spirit be with you all," the doxology, "Praise God from whom all blessings flow, praise him all creatures here below, praise him above you heavenly host, praise Father, Son, and Holy Ghost," and the benediction, "Almighty God, Father, Son, and Holy Spirit, bless you now and forever," which are all Trinitarian in structure. It has been and continues to be the structure of creeds both ancient and modern. The Nicene and Apostles' Creeds both begin with a paragraph on God the Father who creates the world, followed by a paragraph on the Son, Jesus Christ, and conclude with a paragraph on the Holy Spirit. It is the organizing principle for much of Western Christian theology. On the other hand, many Western Christians have focused theology and faith on the person of Jesus to the exclusion of any other theological categories. For these believers the doctrine of the Trinity does not function at all. God's relationship to creation is so narrowed to Jesus that locating God anywhere else in the world is not possible. Other Western Christians use the doctrine of the Trinity in worship and repeat the confession of faith using one of the historical creeds but do not see any relationship between these statements and how God relates to the world salvifically, in a saving manner. The doctrine of the Trinity has become divorced from the doctrine of salvation, soteriology; from the doctrine of the church, ecclesiology; and from how Christians understand what it means for Jesus to be the Christ, christology. Strangest of all is that this doctrine has been separated from the Christian understanding of God. It functions above or alongside of these other doctrines but does not integrate them into a whole, so that it is possible to develop a new doctrine of the Church or Christ without any effect upon the doctrine of the Trinity. Also, since the integration of

1

theology by trinitarian doctrine is purely formal the individual doctrines lose much of their interdependence.

Thus theology in the Western Christian tradition has become disjointed, and the Trinity has become an abstract concept that seems to say something about God but does not affect any other Christian doctrines. For most believers this disjunction is so great as to make them wonder why, aside from tradition, theologians insist on speaking of the Trinity at all. That many theologians have not sensed this need to relate theology to the Trinity also indicates the breadth of the divorce.

How did this situation develop? The West used Latin as its primary language instead of Greek, which meant that theologians like Augustine, who could not read Greek, could only appeal to such Latin authors as Tertullian for insight from the tradition. Thus after Augustine, who developed his own theology, the Western tradition and the Eastern tradition moved in increasingly different directions. Augustine did develop a doctrine of the Trinity, but for him it was a received doctrine for which he was to provide explanation; it was never the central focus for his own theology, nor was it the doctrine that integrated his understanding of Christ, salvation, and how God was related to salvation. The separation of the Trinity from the rest of Christian theology began with Augustine and continued in the Western tradition.

In terms of ecumenical dialogues between Eastern and Western Christians this difference became acute. The Eastern tradition maintained the connectedness between the Trinity and the theology of the Church, which is why the East insists upon the Trinity as what is necessary in order to witness to the Church as Christian. The Western tradition did not maintain this coherence, and instead focused on Jesus as the Christ, viewing the Trinity as a separate issue. Even today the dialogue partners often speak past each other.

One solution to this problem would be for the West simply to adopt Eastern theology, but this would mean adopting a theology that has been characterized by Western theologians as Pelagian or Semi-Pelagian. When Western theologians use these terms they mean to imply that it is necessary for us to do something to experience salvation, so that salvation is not granted by God's grace as an unmerited gift. It would also mean accepting a doctrine of the Trinity in which threeness is primary and adopting a tradition that at this time does not ordain women or entertain language issues related to God. Therefore this is an unlikely solution.

The more realistic solution that this book describes is for the Western Christian to rediscover the original function of the doctrine of the Trinity as integrating soteriology, christology, and the doctrine of God, and to develop a doctrine that will reauthenticate the Trinity. In order for us to understand how the Trinity can be the integrative doctrine for Christian theology it will be necessary to examine the Eastern tradition where it continues to function in that way. This examination will focus on soteriology and christology to see how they are integrated in the Eastern doctrine of the Trinity. The goal is to integrate these doctrines in a doctrine of the Trinity for the West.

As the original doctrine of the Trinity was indebted to the philosophical vocabulary and thought of its time and so was authentic to its context, so a reauthenticated doctrine of the Trinity will be indebted to a contemporary philosophical worldview, namely process philosophy. A process metaphysic presents God and the world as truly related in a salvific way. Its doctrine of God includes the whole world from subatomic particles to human beings in a relationship in which salvation occurs. Thus process thought will help in developing a reauthenticated Trinity that integrates the salvation of the world with God.

The need is for a doctrine of the Trinity that functions for the West as Trinitarian thought has always functioned in the East. Hence the first resource for a reauthenticated Western doctrine is the classical trinitarian teaching of the Eastern Church. The theologian who has done most to recover this Eastern thinking for the West is Jürgen Moltmann. He has rejected the extreme monotheism of the West and has provided a trinitarian alternative that integrates doctrines of christology and salvation, but he emphasizes the threeness to such an extent that this solution may move too suddenly away from the Western concern for unity in God. Feminist theology, although little aware of the Eastern tradition, has recovered a holistic and integrated understanding of salvation that is needed for an adequate Western doctrine of the Trinity. Thus the resources within the Christian tradition that are available for this project are Orthodoxy, Moltmann's work, feminism, and process thought.

Orthodoxy is the theology of the pre-Augustinian tradition of the Christian Church that is currently still practiced in the Eastern Orthodox Christian churches. This tradition formulates the Trinity as its central doctrine, integrating soteriology and christology. So the function which the Trinity is to have in Christian theology will be based upon this Eastern tradition. Thus the Trinity as Father, Son, and Holy Spirit is indicative of an understanding of salvation for which the paradigm is transfiguration. As Jesus was transfigured on Mount Tabor (Mark 9:2-8; Matt 17:1-8; Luke 9:28-36) so all people have the possibility for that same experience. This is because we are created in the image of God, which means that the grace of God is internal to our human nature and defines who we are. It also means that the task that we are invited to undertake is to realize that image by revealing God's love for the world through our own words and deeds.

Thus to sin is to refuse God's invitation to participate in salvation. This gradual process of personally becoming God by grace also contributes to the salvation of the world around us. As the presence of God in us by grace makes our transfiguration possible, so our positive response to that grace transfigures the whole world into the kingdom of God. This understanding of salvation points to God's persuasive manner of relating to the world in order to accomplish salvation which in scope includes not only human persons but also the world.

Jesus is identified as Son in order to indicate the close connection between him and the Father so that what is revealed in the Son is trustworthy. This Christ of God is the leaven in the loaf as we are in the world. In this case because Christ is truly God and truly human, the humanity is transfigured by the presence of divinity in that humanity, and so this Son provides the understanding of the goal of humanity—becoming God by grace—as well as the means by which this is possible. Without the previous transfiguration of the Son humanity would not know of the possibility, and without the actuality of the Son human transfiguration would not be metaphysically possible.

As the Father is present within the world, and the Son is present in the person called Jesus, so the Holy Spirit is present within each believer providing faith and perseverance to follow the Way of God, making it possible for all baptized people to achieve *theosis* (deification), that is, to become God by grace and in that process bring about the salvation of the world. Thus this Trinity of Father, Son, and Holy Spirit are necessary, and are necessary in these categories, in order for salvation to occur in this way. This first Trinity provides a pattern to follow in integrating salvation, Christ, and God into a summary formula.

The second resource is the work of Jürgen Moltmann. Moltmann provides much that agrees with Orthodoxy, especially his understanding that the Trinity includes christology and soteriology as foundational. He adds to these ancient ideas the reciprocal relationship between God and the world so that the "economic Trinity" receives what occurs, what happens in the world. He also adds the notion that time, and therefore change, are at the heart of the universe. Since the "economic Trinity" is the history of salvation, time and change are included in God as well. These ideas plus those of Orthodoxy will inform our own formulation of the doctrine of the Trinity.

The third resource available to this project is feminism. Feminism links our being created in the image of God to our involvement in the process of salvation. Feminism understands salvation in a way that emphasizes the interrelatedness of everything in the world, cooperation between God and human beings, and salvation as something that occurs here and now and includes the whole creation. It redefines sin as obstruction of the process of salvation by refusing to participate, thus denying salvation not only to oneself but also to the world. Sin is against the world and thereby also against God. Feminism calls into question previous images and language about God since those images have been used to exclude women from leadership roles in the Church and, by extension, from power in the political realm as well. It judges these traditional images to be exclusive, limiting, and therefore inadequate. With respect to christology feminists emphasize the Christ as the presence of God in the world in a way that is not limited to Jesus, although God is surely present in him. This emphasis makes it possible to include women as well as men as ones in whom God is present. For feminists the relationship between God and persons is not one of power-over and judgment but one of friendship and cooperation. The goal is not to control others but to free them to respond to God as they are able. God relates to the world in a way that is persuasive. It is also salvific, and it draws upon women's experience of God and of the world and of God in the world.

It is important to note that the feminist view of the world has much in common with Moltmann and Orthodoxy. Salvation occurs here and now, and it is a process of transformation of the world we have now into the world alive with God. Salvation involves the whole world because everything is interrelated with everything else; human beings are created in the image of God and therefore are related to God in a way that makes synergy or cooperation possible and necessary for salvation; sin is refusal to participate in the process of salvation and thereby hinders it, so that to sin against the world is to sin against God; Christ is the evidence of transfiguration or transformation; God relates to the world in a way that is persuasive.

Process thought and specifically process theology is the other resource available to this project. Process theology concurs with the above summary paragraph in all of its conclusions. What process has to offer that has not been heretofore available is a metaphysics that describes how the whole world works with God as an integral part of the process. From a process perspective salvation is an ongoing, persuasive, reciprocal process between God and the world which moves toward harmony in God and toward harmony in the world. Salvation depends upon the persuasive agency of God to involve people in participating in this process. Since the whole cosmos is included, no human endeavor is unrelated to salvation. Human participation can result in the transformation of the world from its current situation into one that is harmonious by means of persons cooperating with the attractiveness of God who lures us into a salvific vision of the future. This process is reciprocal in that God provides the possible futures calling us to actualize the best one. By choosing one of these we prevent the others from being actualized. In response to this choice, God then provides a new set of possible futures from which choices are again made. If our choices enhance harmony, then God and the world rejoice. If our choices result in discord, then God reconciles all that can be reconciled and submits the results to the world. In this view it is possible to have suffering in God as well as in the world because God experiences what we experience, only with greater intensity.

The concluding chapter constructs a doctrine of the Trinity out of these resources. To do so it sketches a distinctive view of Christ and salvation that leads to a quite new doctrine of the Trinity in which the internal relations are not the classical ones. This doctrine is informed by the Eastern tradition but it also exhibits the Western concern to avoid tritheism. In continuity with the Eastern tradition in terms of its function, but breaking with its patriarchal language, the resultant Trinity is named Lover, Christ, and Spirit.

Chapter One

The Development of the Doctrine of the Trinity

The doctrine of the Trinity developed in response to the need of the Christian Church to articulate how Jesus as the Christ is related to God. Since the first Christians had been Jews the commitment to God as one was strong. The problem became: how can Christians witness to the presence of God which they experience in Jesus Christ and still maintain their belief in God as one? As Christian theologians still do, these men consulted the Scriptures to see if they would be a resource. The word Trinity does not appear in the Scriptures but there are several texts that were appealed to in the development of this doctrine.

First, the letters of Paul include greetings at the beginning that, while not trinitarian, do include reference to God as Father and Christ as Lord. These letters are the oldest documents in the New Testament. For example, in Rom 1:7b Paul writes, "Grace to you and peace from God our Father and the Lord Jesus Christ."[1] This same greeting occurs in Paul's letters, including 1 and 2 Corinthians, Galatians, Philippians, Philemon, as well as those letters attributed to Paul such as 1 and 2 Timothy and Titus. Chronologically the next reference is in the gospel of Mark 13:35, "But about that day and hour no one knows, neither the angels in heaven, nor the Son, but only the Father." This text also appears in Matthew, Luke, and Acts. The only direct statement of what became the language of the Trinity is in chapter 28 of Matthew where it is written, "Go therefore and make disciples of all nations, baptizing them in the name of the Father and of the Son and of the

---

[1] All Scripture citations are from the *New Oxford Annotated Bible with the Apocrypha* (NRSV), eds. Bruce Metzger and Roland Murphy (New York: Oxford University Press, 1991) unless otherwise noted.

Holy spirit, and teaching them to obey everything that I have commanded you" (Matt 28:19). The gospel of John makes more references to God as Father and Jesus as Son than do the other gospels. It also makes more references to the Spirit. In terms of the relationships between the three, the Gospel of John notes that the Spirit proceeds from the Father (15:26), the Son is sent by the Father (17:3, 8, 18, 21, 23, 25) and the Spirit is sent by Jesus into the world (15:26-27). Also in John the intimacy between the Father, the Son, and the believers is stated, especially in 17:21-22, "As you, Father, are in me and I am in you may they also be in us, so that the world may believe that you have sent me . . . I in them and you in me, that they may become completely one. . . ." In the Christian tradition this relationship of living in one another, when referred to the Trinity, will be called by the Greek world *perichoresis*. Even though the gospel of John is the latest gospel, the clear statement in Matt 28:19 occurs only that one time. These are the primary Scripture texts that theologians will refer to in developing the doctrine of the Trinity.

Along with the Scriptures the early theologians also used the philosophy that was available to them at the time. Thus the thought of Plato can be seen functioning directly or indirectly in the way the theologians construct their arguments and in the vocabulary they employ. Plato constructed the world in two distinct planes. The higher plane consisted of the ideas, forms, and general abstractions. This plane is not directly encountered by us. Rather we encounter these generalizations in specific, concrete events. So when theologians speak of the essence of God they mean that the essence of God is in the higher plane, transcendent, and therefore unknowable. We can only encounter God in the creation, that is, in concrete events in our world. The only way for this to happen is for God to "come down" into the created world so that God can relate directly to us. In order to bring about the salvation of humanity it was necessary for Jesus to bring together both planes. Thus divinity must enter into humanity and Jesus must be truly human and truly divine. For Christians to say that God was in Christ is to claim that this is what happened in the incarnation. God became human. In this system, time in the higher plane is everlasting. It has no end. But time in the lower plane is finite. It began and it will at some distant future come to an end. Likewise everything created in time is also finite and so comes to an end. Therefore the "real world" is the higher plane because it is permanent while the lower plane perishes. In order for the lower plane to have meaning it needs to participate in the eternal, divine plane and by doing so gain immortality. Thus God, divinity, and eternal time are in the higher plane while humanity, creation, and death are in the lower plane. For the early Christian theologians this philosophy and the Scriptures were their primary resources.

This chapter will trace the highlights of the development of the doctrine of the Trinity from the second century to the Cappadocian Fathers. The Arian controversy and the response by Athanasius are at the center of this development. Attention will be focused on the interdependence of the doctrine of the Trinity, understanding what it means for Jesus to be the Christ, christology, and the understanding of salvation. The development is complex because no doctrine arises in isolation from the others and there are several groups, each of whom wanted its perspective to prevail. As we look back at the history of Christianity we tend to assume that in the early Church the diversity that we experience must have been absent. We project a perfect or ideal time when Christians would all have agreed on doctrines. The inclusion of four gospels in the Scripture indicates that some diversity has been part of Christian experience from the beginning and the history of the early Church indicates that the diversity did escalate into battles between clerics who represented different theological positions. The passion for a particular position in the early centuries was at least equal to that of some current zealous groups eager to gain converts. These early centuries are also marked by the attempt of the emperors to unite their broad empire under one religion. That religion would become Christianity in the early fourth century. The emperors considered themselves guardians of the faith and so took sides in the theological disputes, influencing the outcomes. It was the emperors who called the councils of bishops to meet and make decisions regarding the doctrine of the Church, so that the push to develop doctrine came from outside the Church and initially for a political purpose. This was a complex and risky climate in which to develop doctrine, but that was the task set before these early Christian theologians.

The beginning of the struggle was based in the attempt to articulate the faith of the Church that Jesus was the Christ of God and at the same time maintain that there is only one God. Polytheism, the belief that there are many gods, was rejected as pagan. The theologians who advocated a strict monotheism, belief in only one God, were called Monarchians. They insisted on this position in order to protect the transcendence and oneness of God. By transcendence they meant that God was above the world and related to it as its creator and that God was not affected by what happens in the world. They defended God's monarchy in two different ways. First there were theologians who affirmed the divine monarchy by denying the divinity of Christ. Jesus is then the adopted Son of God, or he has received the power of God at the time of his baptism. Prior to his baptism, he is like every other human being except that he is virtuous. The second form of monarchianism is also called modalism because the oneness of God is maintained by identifying Christ with God the Father so that there is no distinction between the two. Thus Noetus claimed that "Christ was the Father himself, and that the Father himself was born, and suffered and died."[2] Thus there is no real distinction between the Father and the Son. There is only one God who takes on different names and roles as necessary.

Sabellius is the one usually identified with a somewhat more sophisticated expression of the modalistic position. He expressed his understanding of God as being of one substance but having three modes of operation. First, God is revealed as creator and named Father; second, God is revealed as savior and named Son; and third, God is revealed as sanctifier, one who makes things holy, and named Spirit. "Thus there is no difference, save that of appearance and chronological location, between the three entities in question."[3]

These developments in the second and third centuries led to the Arian controversy in the early fourth century. Arius, for whom the controversy was named, was a presbyter (priest) in Alexandria who attracted a following. Arius affirmed the complete and absolute transcendence of the one God. Given this, it followed that the Son must be a creature, the highest of creatures certainly, but a creature nonetheless. Since the Son was a creature he came into existence at a point in time, so that "there was a time when he was not." This means that the Son cannot be of the same or even of a similar essence with the Father. It also means that the Son is subject to change as are all other creatures and so also liable to sin or to decide not to be the Christ. While Arius does speak of a holy Triad he does so in terms that clearly mean that the three are totally different and in no way share the same essence.[4]

Following from the Son being a creature is the corollary that God as Father must have existed alone prior to the creation of the Son. This leads to what is termed subordinationism. The Father is God, whereas the Son is not God but is the highest of creatures. The exact position of the Son is difficult to estimate. He is like all other creatures in being created, yet he is the firstborn of all creation, which gives him a rank that is not shared by other creatures. He also is the Logos. However, this Logos is not essentially (true) God. This ambiguity leads to different evaluations of Arius's thought. Many writers find that the Son is neither divine, because he is created, nor human, because he is the firstborn created by God out of nothing. Thus he is a unique creature that does not have the power to save since he is not divine, nor can he save humanity because he is not truly human

    [2] J. G. Davies, *The Early Christian Church* (Grand Rapids: Baker Book House, 1989) 138.

    [3] Alister E. McGrath, *Christian Theology,* (Cambridge: Basil Blackwell, 1994) 256.

    [4] J. N. D. Kelly, *Early Christian Doctrines* (San Francisco: Harper & Row, 1960) 229.

either. While Arius can establish the absolute transcendence of God and the uniqueness of the Son, he has difficulty showing how the Son assures salvation for humanity.

The latest discussion of Arius by Robert Gregg and Dennis Groh argues that Arius was in fact concerned with salvation, and this leads to a different evaluation of his thought. They claim that for Arius the Son is completely human and is considered divine because of his complete obedience to the will of the Father. This is at least consistent with what is necessary from Arius's perspective for salvation to occur. Arius wants salvation to be available to all people, so what is required must be possible for all people. Therefore what is required is obedience to the will of the Father. Since Jesus was completely obedient to the Father's will, and since he was completely human as we are, we must also be able to be obedient in the same way and enjoy salvation. It was necessary in this perspective for Jesus to be a creature in order to insure this possibility for everyone. It was not necessary for him to be "God" since salvation is by imitation, which all human beings have the power to achieve.

When Arius writes about the Trinity he is clear that the three hypostases, i.e., concrete instances, are described as "separate in nature . . . estranged, unconnected, alien . . . utterly dissimilar from each other with respect to both essences and glories to infinity."[5] Thus Arius maintains a careful hierarchy with the Father identified as divine in a way that the Son and Holy Spirit are not. His doctrine of the Trinity does, however, integrate his understanding of salvation, and of how the Son makes salvation possible for the rest of humanity and who God the Father must be in that understanding. It is this integrative function that the Trinity provides for Christian theology. It even works in the thought of this man, Arius, who would be condemned as a heretic at the Synod of Antioch in February of 325.

In the second century Irenaeus developed the alternative description of salvation that Athanasius used to combat Arius. Irenaeus says that God became human so that humans might become God. This is possible because God became human in the person of Jesus. In that person a divine nature was joined to a human nature so that the human nature is transfigured and the divine nature of Jesus is revealed. The story of the Transfiguration (Mark 9:2-8; Matt 17:1-8; Luke 9:28-36) is the basis for this idea. For those of us who have only human natures, these human natures will be transfigured by the grace of God, so that while Jesus was divine by nature we become divine by grace. Each person will realize this transfiguration differently since each person is unique, but the goal of becoming divine is

    [5] Robert C. Gregg and Dennis Groh, *Early Arianism—A View of Salvation* (Philadelphia: Fortress, 1981) 98.

the same. This transformation begins with baptism when the gift of the Holy Spirit is conferred and continues throughout our lives in communion with the Church and thus with God. Finally, after death, transfiguration becomes complete and we become one with God in the person of the Holy Spirit.

Athanasius was convinced that Arius's Christ who is a creature makes salvation at least uncertain if not impossible. But salvation for Athanasius required that the divine, that is, God, be joined with the not-divine, i.e., the creation, including humanity, in order to transform the not-divine into the divine by grace. This participation of the divine in the human guaranteed salvation in a way that Arius's theology did not. If as Arius taught Jesus could grow in grace, learn, or more importantly change his mind and decide not to be the Christ, then Arius made salvation uncertain because Jesus might have rejected God's will since Jesus was only a creature. Thus the certainty that Athanasius required, which was vested in the category of the divine nature, not the category of will, was not possible the way Arius described salvation.

Athanasius determines that in order to insure salvation Christ must be divine by nature, must originate divinely so that he cannot change, and must be obedient to follow God's will completely because he cannot do otherwise. So Athanasius insists that the Son is *"homoousios"* (of the same essence) with the Father because this is necessary to insure that salvation will happen. "If the first Son is not Son by nature then we cannot participate in this Son by the Spirit and become daughters and sons of God."[6] The same participation is necessary from the human side as well. If Christ was not truly human then we are not saved, because only that which is assumed is saved. Thus Christ's humanity in Jesus is equally necessary to make our participation in God possible. It was Athanasius' concern for the salvation of the world that moved him steadfastly to defend the *"homoousion"* of the Son and to expand the *"homoousion"* to the Holy Spirit as well. What began as a problem in how salvation is possible in Jesus Christ developed into the doctrine of the Trinity.

This idea of the Trinity begins with the salvation of the world as its goal and attempts to explain how God is related to the world so as to make this salvation described in terms of participation possible. The language employed needed to distinguish between the divine nature of God (the *ousia,* essence) and the concrete instances of the presence of God as experienced in the world (the *hypostases,* persons). Both the essence and the *hypostases* are fully God. Otherwise the presence of the second person of the

---

[6] Frances Young, *From Nicaea to Chalcedon* (London: S.C.M., 1983) 72.

Trinity, Christ, would not bring about salvation. That salvation is brought about by God as Trinity indicates the true nature of God as trinitarian and is not a response to the need for salvation to occur in a certain way.

At the Synod in Alexandria in 362 Athanasius proposed that the formula "three *hypostases*" (concrete instances) was legitimate providing that it was understood not to mean "three essences" *(ousias),* different in essence, but "merely expressed the separate subsistence of the three Persons in the consubstantial *(homoousion)* Triad."[7] This was sufficient to allay the fears of those who thought "three *hypostases*" really meant "three *ousias*" and thus three gods. Soon after this synod the Roman Empire split into East and West. The West retained the *"homoousion"* position, but the East continued to be challenged by the Arians and by an emperor who supported them.

The Cappadocian Fathers

The supporters of the *"homoousion"* cause in the East were led by Basil of Caesarea, his brother, Gregory of Nyssa, and his friend, Gregory Nazianzus. The contribution of these Cappadocian Fathers is summarized by Alexander Schmemann: "They perfected the creation of a theological language, crystallized its concepts, and expressed all the profound significance of the orthodox doctrine of the Holy Trinity contained in Athanasius' *homoousion* and in the Nicene Creed."[8] Following is a description of their contributions to the development of the doctrine of the Trinity in the Eastern Christian tradition. This section will focus on the vocabulary that was employed by the Cappadocian Fathers in order to convince those who did not share their orthodox position and to support the role they assigned to the Holy Spirit, which was not defined until the First Council of Constantinople in 381 C.E.

Basil was the eldest of the three and thus he began serving the Church and writing earlier than the others. It was in 360, prior to the last synod, that he stated his opinion of the *"homoiousion."* He said, "If I must give my own view it is this. The phrase 'like in essence' *(homoiousion),* if it be read with the addition 'without any difference,' I accept as conveying the same sense as the *homoousion.* . . . But if any one cuts off the qualification 'without any difference' from the word 'like,' as was done at Constantinople [360 C.E.] then I regard the phrase with suspicion, as derogatory to the dignity of the Only-begotten. We are frequently accustomed to entertain the idea of 'likeness' in the case of indistinct resemblances, coming anything

---

[7] Kelly, *Early Christian Doctrines* 254.

[8] Alexander Schmemann, *The Historical Road of Eastern Orthodoxy* (New York: St. Vladimir's Seminary Press, 1963) 93.

but close to the originals. I am myself for the *homoousion,* as being less open to improper interpretation."[9]

Basil understood the importance of the word *"homoousion"* for preventing Arianism, and he knew its history, which he explains in a letter written in 370 C.E. He uses the illustration of two coins, both of which are made of copper, which implies the existence of the substance called copper. However, this analogy with the Godhead becomes incorrect if it assumes a substance either prior to God or somehow underlying God. This assumption accounts for the rejection of the word at the Synod of 268. Basil also rejects that understanding of *homoousion* and understands the Council of Nicaea to have meant "of the same stuff" by the *homoousion.*[10] Thus Nicaea wished to express the view that "whatever the Father is the Son is also in identical measure."[11] Against the Arian position "the term *homoousion* was adopted to extirpate the impiety. For the conjunction of the Son with the Father is without time and without interval . . . when both the cause and that which derives its natural existence from the cause are of the same nature, then they are called 'of one substance.'"[12]

Basil also interprets *homoousion* as a safeguard against Sabellianism in that for two entities to be *homoousios* they must be distinct in order to be compared. Something cannot be *homoousios* with itself. It is possible to be distinct without being separate. So for the East being distinct does not mean being separate and thus does not compromise the unity of God.

Related to *homoousion* are two other words which also caused considerable confusion. They are *ousia* and *hypostasis.* According to G. L. Prestige *"ousia* tends to regard internal characteristics and relations, or metaphysical reality; while hypostasis regularly emphasizes the externally concrete character of the substance, or empirical objectivity."[13] Sensing the confusion these terms were causing, Basil, the elder brother, wrote to his younger brother Gregory concerning the difference between *ousia* and *hypostasis,*

> Many persons, in their study of the sacred dogmas, failing to distinguish between what is common in the essence or substance, and the meaning of the *hypostasis,* arrive at the same notions, and think that it makes no difference whether *ousia* or *hypostasis* be spoken of. The result is that some of those who accept statements on these subjects without any enquiry, are pleased to speak of "one *hypostasis,*" just as they do of one "essence" or "substance"; while on the other hand those who accept three *hypostases* are under the

---

[9] Basil, Letter IX, to Maximus the Philosopher, *NPNF* 4:123.

[10] G. L. Prestige, *God in Patristic Thought* (London: S.P.C.K., 1952) 203.

[11] Basil, Letter LII, *NPNF* ser. 2, 4:155.

[12] Basil, Letter LII, 156 (ca. 370 C.E.).

[13] Prestige, *God in Patristic Thought* 188.

idea that they are bound in accordance with this confession to assert also, by numerical analogy, three essences or substances.[14]

Those who confessed three substances, essences *(ousias)* or ideas as well as three *hypostases* were the Arians. Those who "speak of one *hypostasis*" just as they do of one "essence" are primarily Western Christians who are then "compelled to confess only three persons and, in their hesitation to speak of three *hypostases,* are convicted of failure to avoid the error of Sabellius, for even Sabellius . . . by asserting that the same *hypostasis* changed its form to meet the needs of the moment, does endeavor to distinguish Persons."[15]

To an Eastern Christian the use of the term "person" meant *persona* in Greek, and the *persona* was the mask that players wore on stage so that they could play more than one part in a play. So *persona* meant a mask only and did not denote a separate *hypostasis* or a different player. Basil makes several attempts to clarify this issue. The coin example in Letter CCXXXXVI is a very early statement, about 360 C.E. In Letter XXXVIII he says, "That which is spoken of in a special and peculiar manner is indicated by the name of the *hypostasis.* . . . This then is the *hypostasis* or *'understanding'*; not the indefinite conception of the essence or substance, which because what is signified as general, finds not *'standing'* but the conception which by means of the expressed peculiarities gives *standing* and circumscription to the general and uncircumscribed."[16]

The operative philosophy in Gregory's thought is Platonic. The relation between *ousia* and *hypostasis* is the relation between an "idea" and its concrete instance in the world. Thus *hypostasis* is an "understanding" because the world in which it exists stands under the higher realm of the forms or ideas. That these terms required explanation was evident as early as 360 when Basil wrote to Gregory. That this is a source of the problem between East and West is indicated in Letter CCXIV written in 375 C.E. This involves these same words and also shows the difference between the Greek and Latin languages on this issue:

> The non-identity of *hypostasis* and *ousia* is, I take it, suggested even by our western brethren, where, from a suspicion of the inadequacy of their own language, they have given the word *ousia* in the Greek to the end that any possible difference of meaning might be preserved in the clear and unconfounded distinction of terms. . . . I shall state that *ousia* has the same relation to *hypostasis* as the common has to the particular . . . . the term *ousia* is common, like goodness, or Godhead, or any similar attribute; while

---

[14] Basil, Letter XXXVIII, *NPNF* ser. 2, 4:137 (ca. 360–362).
[15] Basil, Letter CCXXXVI, *NPNF* ser. 2, 4:278. (ca. 376).
[16] Basil Letter XXXVIII, *NPNF* ser. 2, 4:138.

> *hypostasis* is contemplated in the special property of Fatherhood, Sonship or the power to sanctify. If then they describe the Persons as being without *hypostasis,* the statement is *per se* absurd; but if they concede that the Persons exist in real *hypostasis* . . . let them so reckon them that the principle of the *homoousion* may be preserved in the unity of the Godhead.[17]

The difference in the languages is at least partially responsible for the misunderstanding. The problem is that Latin contains no word that is actually equivalent to *hypostasis.* Therefore in being translated into Latin from Greek both *ousia* and *hypostasis* became *substantia,* "substance." Latin could not distinguish between the two terms. So the Latin-speaking West returned to the formula of Tertullian, who had proposed that there is one "substance" in three "persons."

While this discussion was initiated as a problem in christology, that is, the Son is *homoousios* with the Father, Basil now is including the Holy Spirit, "the power that sanctifies" as also *homoousios,* although he refrains from actually saying that the Spirit is *homoousios.* In giving account of the faith he writes,

> We must, therefore, confess the faith by adding the particular to the common. The Godhead is common; the fatherhood particular. We must therefore combine the two and say, "I believe in God the Father." The like course must be pursued in the confession of the Son; we must combine the particular with the common and say, "I believe in God the Son," so in the case of the Holy Ghost we must make our utterance conform to the appellation and say, "I believe in God the Holy Ghost."[18]

Basil considers any hierarchy in the Godhead unacceptable, as well as any notion that Christ is the source of the Spirit. Both of these possibilities were available. For example, the first creed of Sirmium stated, "the Paraclete, Whom He sent as He promised to the Apostles after His ascent to heaven"[19] indicates that the Spirit is sent by the Son but does not make clear the origin of the Spirit. The Second Creed of Sirmium is equally confusing. It says, "but the Paraclete, the Spirit, is through the Son."[20] The Creed of Constantinople (360 C.E.) is very similar: "'The Spirit of Truth,' Whom He sent to them when He had ascended to heaven."[21] The ambiguity of these statements apparently was not an issue for Western Christians but it did raise questions for the Eastern theologians. If the statements im-

---

[17] Basil, Letter CCXIV, *NPNF* ser. 2, 4:138.
[18] Basil, Letter CCXXXVI, *NPNF* ser. 2, 4:278.
[19] Kelly, *Early Christian Creeds* (New York: Longman, Inc., 1972) 272.
[20] Kelly, *Early Christian Creeds* 286.
[21] Kelly, *Early Christian Creeds* 294.

plied that the Son is the source of the Spirit, then the statements needed to be challenged. Basil set out to clear up the ambiguities. Thus he insists that

> the Holy Spirit is numbered with the Father and the Son, because He is above creation. . . . He is not even anterior, for nothing intervenes between Son and Father. If, however, He is not of God, but is through Christ, He does not exist at all. It follows, that this new invention about the order really involves the destruction of the actual existence, and is a denial of the whole faith. It is equally impious to reduce Him to the level of a creature, and to subordinate Him either to Son or to Father, either in time or in rank."[22]

Basil interprets "through" to indicate the source of the Spirit, which divides the originating principle, the Father, and is therefore unacceptable. The closing sentence refers directly to the Second Creed of the Council of Dedication which, while affirming that the names indicated distinct entities, also said "but denoting accurately the peculiar subsistence *[hypostasis]*, rank, and glory of each that is named."[23] This suggests a hierarchy of rank or importance, and Basil is clear that God is God and cannot be set up in some hierarchy. Basil offered a solution to the problem of understanding the Trinity so that all Three are equal or of the same essence and yet distinct in their particularity. He writes, "we do not speak of the Holy Ghost as unbegotten, for we recognize one Unbegotten and one Origin of all things, the Father of our Lord Jesus Christ: nor do we speak of the Holy Ghost as begotten, for by the tradition of the faith we have been taught one Only-begotten: the Spirit of truth we have been taught to proceed from the Father and we confess Him to be of God without creation."[24]

Gregory of Nyssa, faced with the same problem, offers a more philosophically based argument, but the object is still to show that having a plurality or hierarchy in the Godhead is impossible. He argues that "one infinite cannot be greater or less than another. . . . To speak of 'large' and 'small' or 'before' and 'after' introduces compositeness into the single unity of the undivided divine Substance. . . . For Gregory, Father and Son express not so much different Beings as an eternal relationship with one divine Being; for without the Son, the Father has neither existence nor name."[25]

For Gregory the three *hypostases* of the Trinity are all divine, and it is not possible to entertain the notion of more or less divine. Gregory locates the oneness of God in the oneness of the nature of God. The threeness or names of God, Father, Son, and Holy Spirit, refer to the activities of God.

---

[22] Basil, Letter CXXV, *NPNF* ser. 2, 4:195 (ca. 373 C.E.)
[23] Athanasius, *De Synodis, NPNF* ser. 2, 4:461.
[24] Basil, Letter CXXV, *NPNF* ser. 2, 4:195.
[25] Young, *From Nicaea to Chalcedon* 111.

However, these activities, while distinguishable, are not done separately, "but every activity which pervades from God to creation and is named according to our manifold design starts off from the Father, proceeds through the Son and is completed by the Holy Spirit."[26] While in this particular work Gregory is arguing that God is one, he is still careful to maintain the distinctions of the three *hypostases* so that "the principle of cause distinguishes the *hypostases* in the Holy Trinity in worshipping that which is uncaused and the other which is from the cause."[27]

Gregory also attempts to explain the structure of the Trinity by analogy. His analogies, unlike Augustine's analogy of components within one individual mind, use three gold coins and three persons. The gold coins are all gold and are referred to in the singular when described as gold. However, when used in the plural gold is intended to refer to the coins themselves, so that "it is not the material but the small coins that receive the significance of the number."[28] "Therefore just as the golden staters are many but the gold is one, thus those who are individually in the nature of man are revealed as many, for example Peter, James and John. But the 'man' in them is one."[29] Thus humanity is the universal and the persons of Peter, James, and John are the concrete, particular instances of humanity.

Gregory wants to establish that God is indivisible in essence and eternally in relationship among the individual *hypostases.* He is also faced with being accused by some believers of profanity for considering the Holy Spirit to be divine. This same response also addresses the attempt to formulate the Godhead with a hierarchy. He says in his treatise *On the Holy Spirit,* "we confess that the Holy Spirit is of the same rank as the Father and the Son, so that there is no difference between them in anything to be thought or named, that devotion can ascribe to a Divine nature."[30] Again in *On the Faith* he writes on behalf of the Church, "the Church believes, as concerning the Son, so equally concerning the Holy Spirit that He is uncreated, and that the whole creation becomes good by participation in the good which is above it, while the Holy Spirit needs not any to make Him good . . . every excellent attribute is predicated of the Father and of the Son. . . . Thus where the Father and the Son are understood to be, there the Holy Spirit also is understood to be."[31]

---

[26] Gregory of Nyssa, "Concerning We Should Think of Saying that There Are Not Three Gods to Ablabius," in *The Trinitarian Controversy,* tr. Wm. Rusch (Philadelphia: Fortress, 1980) 155.

[27] Ibid. 160, 161.

[28] Ibid. 158.

[29] Ibid.

[30] Gregory of Nyssa, *On the Holy Spirit, NPNF* ser. 2, 5:315 (377 C.E.).

[31] Gregory of Nyssa, *On the Faith, NPNF* ser. 2, 5:338 (375 C.E.).

Gregory is asserting that the Trinity always operates together. While each has a particular role assigned they do not act separately; therefore there is one God. "Thus the identity of the operation in Father, Son and Holy Spirit shows plainly the undistinguishable character of their substance *(ousia)*."[32]

For Gregory the *ousia* or essence itself is beyond human knowing. God in Trinity is internally related to the world in that God permeates the whole world and yet the essence of God remains unknowable. In fact, for Gregory these two belong together:

> If anyone should ask for some interpretation and description, and explanation of the Divine Essence, we are not going to deny that in this kind of wisdom, we are unlearned, acknowledging only so much as this, that it is not possible that that which is by nature infinite should be comprehended in any conception expressed by words. . . . For nothing is Divine that is conceived as being circumscribed, but it belongs to the Godhead to be in all places and to pervade all things and not to be limited by anything.[33]

This pervading of God in the world is the basis for participation of humans in God. All three members of the Trinity are necessary for this participation, which is salvation understood as divinization, or in Greek *theosis,* which is the becoming God by grace described first by Irenaeus. In order for salvation in this manner to be possible the Trinity constructed in this way is necessary. "As it is impossible to mount to the Father unless our thoughts are exalted thither through the Son, so it is impossible also to say that Jesus is Lord except by the Holy Spirit. Therefore Father, Son and Holy Spirit are to be known only in a perfect Trinity, in closest consequence and union with each other, before all creation, before all ages, before any thing whatever of which we can form an idea."[34]

Thus Gregory is also concerned to contribute to the understanding of the Holy Spirit. He does not use "proceed" as does Basil and as Gregory Nazianzus will, but he contributes the notion of the Holy Spirit as "life-giving": "then again He [Holy Spirit] is so by virtue of life-giving . . . of capacity to give all good things, and above them all life itself, and by being everywhere, being present in each, filling the earth, residing in the heavens, shed abroad upon supernatural Powers, filling all things according to the deserts of each . . . and yet not parted from the Holy Trinity."[35]

To the more mystical and philosophical theology of Gregory of Nyssa is now to be added the theology of Gregory Nazianzus, the theologian. It

---

[32] Gregory of Nyssa, *On the Trinity, NPNF* ser. 2, 5:329 (380 C.E.).

[33] Gregory of Nyssa, *Against Eunomius,* Book III, *NPNF* ser. 2, 5:146.

[34] Gregory of Nyssa, *On the Holy Spirit, NPNF* ser. 2, 5:319 (377 C.E.).

[35] Gregory of Nyssa, *On the Holy Spirit,* 319.

was up to this Gregory to find a compromise position, to unify the Church, and yet to do it in such a way as to be faithful to Nicaea and to Basil, his friend. Therefore this Gregory was concerned to uphold the divinity of the Holy Spirit and to develop language for describing the internal relations of the Godhead. He is aware of the positions presented by Arianism and Sabellianism and that he needs to find a middle way. He is also concerned to include the Western Church and so includes "person" in a way that implies that it is equal to *hypostasis,* something that Basil had been more reluctant to do. Oration 39, delivered sometime between 379 and 381 C.E., is a good example of Gregory's concerns:

> We would keep equally far from the confession of Sabellius and from the divisions of Arius, which evils are diametrically opposed yet equal in their wickedness. For what need is there heretically to fuse God together, or to cut Him up into inequality? . . . For to us there is but One God, the Father, of Whom are all things; and One Lord Jesus Christ, by Whom are all things; yet these words, of, by, in Whom, do not denote a difference of nature . . . but they characterize the personalities of a nature which is one and unconfused."[36]

He continues to use the vocabulary of Basil and the Eastern Church, attempting to make *ousia* and *hypostasis* acceptable theological terms. Thus "when I speak of God you must be illumined at once by one flash of light and by three. Three in Individualities or Hypostases, if any prefer to call them, or persons, for we will not quarrel about names so long as the syllables amount to the same meaning; but One in respect of the Substance—that is the Godhead."[37]

In his attempt to find language to express the distinction or origination in the Godhead Gregory claims to coin a word, although Basil had in fact used the word some ten years earlier. Gregory writes: "The Holy Ghost is truly Spirit, coming forth from the Father, indeed, but not after the manner of the Son, for it is not by Generation but by Procession (since I must coin a word for the sake of clearness). . . ."[38]

Gregory appeals to Scripture, John 15:26, to support his choice of the word "proceeds." John 15:26 reads, "But when the Counselor comes, whom I shall send to you from the Father, even the Spirit of truth, who proceeds from the Father, he will bear witness to me."[39] As far as the East is concerned this scriptural quotation settles the debate. It says "who proceeds from the Father," and that is sufficient.

---

[36] Gregory Nazianzus, Oration 39, *NPNF* ser. 2, 7:356.

[37] Gregory Nazianzus, Oration 39, 355.

[38] Gregory Nazianzus, Oration 39, 356.

[39] RSV. The NRSV changes the word "proceeds" to "comes," thus obscuring the historical connection.

Gregory understood the problem affiliated with the terminology, especially the difficulty in going from Greek to Latin. He took the opportunity to explain the Eastern position during his treatise *On the Great Athanasius*.

> We use in an orthodox sense the terms one Essence and Three *Hypostases,* the one to denote the nature of the Godhead, and the other the properties of the Three; the Italians mean the same, but owing to the scantiness of their vocabulary, and its poverty of terms, they are unable to distinguish between Essence and *Hypostasis* and therefore introduce the term Persons, to avoid being understood to assert three Essences. The result, were it not piteous, would be laughable. This slight difference of sound was taken to indicate a difference of faith. Then, Sabellianism was suspected in the doctrine of Three Persons, Arianism in that of Three *Hypostases,* both being the offspring of a contentious spirit. . . . He [Athanasius] conferred in his gentle and sympathetic way with both parties, and after he had carefully weighed the meaning of their expressions, and found that they had the same sense, and were nowise different in doctrine, by permitting each party to use its own terms, he bound them together in unity of action.[40]

This doctrine of the Trinity was developed on the basis of the understanding of salvation provided by Irenaeus and Athanasius. Thus this is the Trinity that undergirds and summarizes salvation as deification *(theosis)*. The *homoousion* is necessary in order to make it possible for humans to become deified. Since Jesus Christ joined the divine nature to the human nature it is now possible for humans to become divine, not by nature, but by grace. The development of the divinity of the Holy Spirit was necessary because it is only by means of the Holy Spirit that one has the grace necessary to have faith in Christ as the Son. Recognizing the Christ as the Son of God makes it possible for one to know the Father who begets the Son and from whom the Holy Spirit proceeds. This process is necessary in order for us to understand that it is the presence of God that permeates the whole creation, including human persons. Since this is true, then, we who are created in the image of God are able to realize this image by participation in God in the person *(hypostasis)* of the Holy Spirit. Thus this whole Trinity understood in this way is necessary for humans to become God by grace. The concrete statement of this Trinity is expressed in the Nicene Creed adopted at Constantinople in 381.

Conclusion

Gregory went to the council in Constantinople in 381 to bring unity to the Church. This council was called by the Emperor Theodosius "to seal

---

[40] Gregory Nazianzus, *On the Great Athanasius, NPNF* ser. 2, 7:279.

the triumph of the Nicene position."[41] It was at this council that Gregory Nazianzus preached the Last Farewell (Oration XLII), since he felt compelled to resign in order to bring peace and unity to the Church. He thought that he was too identified with one side of the discussion, and rather than continue in discord he elected to step aside. So he urges the Church to seek unity.

> Let us then bid farewell to all contentious shiftings and balancings of the truth on either side, neither, like the Sabellians, assailing the Trinity in the interest of the unity and so destroying the distinction by a wicked confusion; nor like the Arians, assailing the Unity in the interest of the Trinity, and by an impious distinction overthrowing the Oneness. . . . But we walking along the royal road which is the seat of virtues . . . believe in the Father, the Son and the Holy Ghost, of one Substance *[ousia]* and glory; in Whom baptism has its perfection . . . acknowledging the Unity in the Essence *[ousia]* and in the undivided worship, and the Trinity in the *Hypostases* or Persons (which term some prefer).[42]

The doctrine put forth in the Creed of Constantinople reaffirmed the use of the term *homoousion* in describing the relationship of the Son to the Father, so the Son is "true God from true God, begotten not made, of one substance with the Father." The emperor Theodosius was a supporter of the Nicene, hence *"homoousion"* position. The work of the Cappadocian Fathers and Athanasius, who had supported this term beginning in 325, was of crucial importance in promoting the *homoousion*.

The Cappadocians wrote in favor of the divinity of the Holy Spirit. The creed of 325 had only mentioned the Holy Spirit but had not noted any functions. Basil was the first to insist on the divinity of the Holy Spirit. Gregory of Nyssa began describing the Spirit as life-giving. Gregory Nazianzus added "proceeds" to describe how the Holy Spirit originates from the Father in a way that is different from the Son. This helped clarify the internal relationships in the Trinity. In the Creed the role of the Holy Spirit is described in a brief paragraph as that of "the Lord and life-giver, Who proceeds from the Father,"[43] all contributions made by the Cappadocian theologians.

These theologians also developed the language that supported the doctrine of the Trinity. Gregory of Nyssa added the philosophical terms and defined them to particularly fit the issue of the Trinity. The Trinity has since been described in the East as three *hypostases* in one *ousia*. Gregory

---

[41] Young, *From Nicaea to Chalcedon* 98.

[42] Gregory Nazianzus, Oration 42, *The Last Farewell, NPNF* ser. 2, 7:90.

[43] Kelly, *Early Christian Creeds* 298.

Nazianzus is credited with providing the compromise which allowed the Church to agree on the creed at this council in Constantinople in 381.

This council was later declared to be the second ecumenical council, the first one being the Council of Nicaea in 325. They are judged to be ecumenical because they were faithful to the doctrine of the Church and the whole Church was represented at these councils. It is this Creed of Constantinople that is confessed today in Eastern and Western churches together under the name of the Nicene Creed. The fact that the Nicene Creed is not exactly the same in the East and in the West indicates a difference in the understanding of the Trinity, in the understanding of salvation and how it is accomplished, and in the role of Christ in salvation. These differences are due primarily to the work of one remarkable theologian in the Western tradition, Augustine.

Chapter Two

The Western Doctrine
of the Trinity

The doctrine of the Trinity developed differently in the Western Christian tradition than in the East because of one primary figure, Augustine of Hippo. This chapter will focus on three major figures: Augustine, Luther, and Calvin. Each theologian's doctrine of the Trinity will be described, together with the relationship of the Trinity to their respective doctrines of christology and salvation.

Augustine

Augustine was a convert to Christianity who developed his theology based on Scripture, received doctrines of the Church, and his own experience. In his earlier writings he was closer to the Platonism of his education, while in his later writings he was much more pessimistic about human possibilities and more certain of human sinfulness. Augustine's assessment of human abilities and limitations influenced his understanding of salvation and what is necessary for it to occur. In his *On Free Choice of the Will,* which he completed in 395 C.E., Augustine located sin and evil in the voluntary free choice of the human will, which is so attracted to this world and bodily pleasures that it is turned away from the eternal good of God (I.28). Since this choice is voluntary, human beings are to be held responsible for choosing temporal things over eternal things. At this time in Augustine's writings he used language of focusing on or being attracted to either good or evil. To focus on one excludes the possibility of seeing the other, and so constitutes a choice for one and against the other.

Augustine argued that humans have been created with the capacity for the highest good, that the creator aids humans in achieving this good, that God will complete and perfect our progress and that those who refuse to strive will be justly condemned.[1] Augustine wrote this text against the Manicheans and so stressed free will as opposed to determinism by the stars, which was a Manichean doctrine. However, in his *Retractions* he stated the position that is more clearly to be seen in his later writings, namely that unless the human will is freed by God's grace from bondage to sin and is thus aided by God it is not possible for human beings to overcome sin and live a pious life.

This addressing of a particular issue in such a specific context led Augustine to apparently contradictory conclusions. We can see this by comparing what he saw as the role of human beings when he was writing for persons being instructed in the faith in preparation for baptism (catechumens) with what he wrote against Pelagius, a British contemporary who was afraid that Augustine's insistence on God electing the saved would lead to moral decay because people would not act morally unless they would be rewarded. In the former writing Augustine assumes that we have the ability to respond positively to God, and he encourages us to do so. However, when he writes against Pelagius, Augustine is clear that God's grace is irresistible and always effective, accomplishing its goal of the salvation of the elect. It is this latter position describing humans as ruined, or a mass of perdition, that requires salvation to be the sovereign election of God in spite of this human condition. This has come to be identified as the mature Augustinian position.

In the *City of God* Augustine states that the elect few are destined to the "perfectly ordered and harmonious enjoyment of God and of one another in God" (19.13). He also describes the eternal punishment of the non-elect in some detail. This position is consistent with what he said in *On The Trinity* 5.16. "Therefore He loved all His saints before the foundation of the world, as He predestined them." This relationship of God to humanity in terms of predestination, while it echoes Paul, is an original contribution of Augustine to Christian theology.

For Augustine all human beings participate in the fall of Adam as stated in the Latin translation of the Scriptures called the Vulgate. This translation of Rom 5:12, which Augustine quotes in *On The Trinity* 4.12, reads "by one man sin entered into the world, and death by sin; and so death passed upon all men, in whom all have sinned."[2] As a result all people are

---

[1] Augustine, *On Free Choice of the Will,* tr. A. S. Benjamin and L. H. Hackstaff (Indianapolis: Bobbs Merrill, 1964) 138.

[2] Augustine, "On the Trinity," *NPNF*, ed. Philip Schaff (Buffalo: The Christian Literature Co., 1887) 3:77.

justly condemned to eternal punishment. But because God is merciful as well as just, God will elect a few to eternal salvation. These few are to replace the angels who fell away from God.[3] For Augustine this is good news, because he is quite convinced if he had been left to his own resolve he would and could never have become a Christian. It was only by God's grace and his mother's persistence (she is clearly God's agent in his conversion according to the *Confessions*) that Augustine was turned from a life of great sinning to being a believer.

How is this possible? Human beings are lost; their will is corrupt and they can do nothing on their own behalf. Yet because God is merciful, God has decided to save a few people. What is necessary to accomplish this task? It is necessary for God to act since humans cannot. But God needs to act in such a way that evil can be defeated and a role model provided. Therefore the Mediator is both human and God. Because he is God he has the power to defeat evil, and because he is human he has the ability to be an archetype for human behavior. Obviously this person is Jesus Christ. Yet Augustine struggled with the concept of God becoming human. He came from a philosophical tradition that emphasized the transcendence, unchangeability, and power of God. In the *Confessions* he refers to Jesus Christ as "a man of marvelous wisdom" (VII. 19. 25). There is still a long step from here to Jesus Christ as divine. However, it is necessary in order for salvation to occur. "For we come to death through sin; He through righteousness . . . therefore as our death is the punishment of sin, so His death was made a sacrifice for sin."[4] For Augustine, Christ's divinity was a given because he is the second Person of the Trinity.

Albert Outler contends that Augustine derived his christology from his doctrine of the Trinity, which was for him a received doctrine of the Church. "This constitutes an important reversal of the pattern of early and patristic Christianity, in which the doctrine of the Trinity is a derivation from the Christian confession of Jesus Christ as Lord and Savior."[5] This reversal may account for the fact that Augustine does not clearly delineate the roles of the Trinity in the event of salvation as the patristic writers did, but speaks of all three persons acting together in a way that makes clear distinctions difficult. It is also consistent with Augustine's soteriology, his understanding of how salvation works. What is necessary, election (God's choice of those who will be saved), has occurred before the foundation of the world. Thus this predestination occurred before Jesus or even Adam;

---

[3] Augustine, *The City of God*, tr. Gerald Walsh, ed. Vernon Bourke (New York: Doubleday, 1958) XII. 22.

[4] "On The Trinity" IV. xii. 77.

[5] Albert Outler, "The Person and Work of Christ," in *A Companion to the Study of St. Augustine,* ed. Roy Battenhouse (Grand Rapids: Baker Book House, 1955) 348.

only the decision of the one God was required. God as Trinity is not necessary to Augustine's understanding of salvation as election, yet this doctrine was already established in the Church, and as a theologian of the Church Augustine took on the task of explaining the doctrine of the Trinity.

Augustine has been the most influential Western theologian in determining the shape of Western trinitarian theology. He wrote *On the Trinity* over a period of seventeen years, finishing the work in 417 C.E. He was carefully explaining one of the Church's doctrines for the edification of believers. His primary sources were Scripture (there are one hundred forty-nine quotations in Book I alone) and Aristotle's *Categories,* which provide the structure for the first eight books of *On The Trinity.* Augustine also had the work on the Trinity by Hilary of Poitiers and refers to it in Books VI, X, XI, and XII. However, he only had Latin translations of excerpts from such theologians as Athanasius, Basil of Caesarea, and Gregory Nazianzus. This he acknowledges in Book III where he says "let them also bear in mind that the writings which we have read on these subjects have not been sufficiently explained in the Latin tongue, or they are not available, or at least it was difficult for us to find them; nor are we so familiar with Greek, as to be in any way capable of reading and understanding such books on these subjects in the language, although from the few excerpts that have been translated for us, I have no doubt that they contain everything that we can profitably seek."[6]

Augustine devotes the first eight Books of *On the Trinity* to discussing Aristotle's ten categories (substance, quantity, quality, relation, place, time, position, state, action, and affection).[7] Having addressed all of these, Augustine determines that only substance and relation apply to God because God transcends all of the others. Therefore he states in *Trin.* V.2, "God as good without quality, as great without quantity, as the Creator who lacks nothing, who rules but from no position, and who contains all things without an external form, as being whole everywhere without limitation of space, as eternal without time, as making mutable things without any change in Himself, and as a Being without passion."[8] This paragraph rules out all but substance and relation, which he continues to employ in his explanation of the Trinity.

Augustine refers to Scripture as the ground for the Trinity as well as for the unity of the Godhead. Thus in *Trin.* XV.28 Augustine writes, "for the

---

[6] Augustine, *The Trinity,* tr. Stephen McKenna, C.S.S.R. (Washington, D.C.: Catholic University of America Press, 1963) 167.

[7] Aristotle, *The Categories: On Interpretation,* by Harold P. Cooke; *Prior Analytics,* by Hugh Tredennick. LCL 325 (London: W. Heinemann, and Cambridge, Mass.: Harvard University Press, 1983) 18.

[8] Augustine, *The Trinity* 285.

Truth would not say, Go, baptize all nations in the name of the Father and of the Son and of the Holy Spirit, unless Thou wast a Trinity. . . . Nor would the divine voice have said, Hear, O Israel, the Lord thy God is one God, unless Thou wert so a Trinity as to be one Lord God."[9] Augustine also appeals to Scripture in support of his understanding that the Spirit proceeds from the Father and the Son. Again in *Trin.* XV.26 he writes :

> And it is proved by many other testimonies of the divine words that He is Spirit of both the Father and the Son, who is specially called the Holy Spirit in the Trinity. The Son Himself likewise says of Him: "Whom I will send you from the Father" (Jn 15.26) and in another place: "Whom the Father will send in my name " (Jn 14.26). But it is so taught that He proceeds from both, because the Son Himself says: "He proceeds from the Father" (Jn 15.26). And when He had risen from the dead and appeared to His disciples, He breathed upon them and said: "Receive the Holy Spirit" (Jn 20.20) in order to show that He also proceeded from Himself. And this is the power "which went forth from him and healed all" (Lk 6.19) as we read in the Gospel.[10]

This is an innovative way to put these Scripture texts together and an original interpretation as well. Augustine is unable to find support in any previous theologian, since

> from the days of Tertullian, the typical formula had been "From the Father through the Son." In the fourth century, however, the deeper implication was extracted from this that the Son, conjointly with the Father, was actually productive of the Holy Spirit. The text to which appeal was regularly made was the Lord's statement in JN 16.14, "He (i.e. the Spirit) will receive of mine." Here the pioneers were St. Hilary (cf. his *Patre et filio auctoribus*) and Marius Victorinus (not St. Ambrose, whose texts refer to the Spirit's *external* mission), but both these avoid speaking directly of His procession from the Son. St. Augustine felt no need of reserve. . . . The logical development of his thought involved the belief that the Holy Spirit proceeded as truly from the Son as from the Father, and he did not scruple to expound it with frankness and precision on many occasions.[11]

The role of the Holy Spirit for Augustine is to be the link or the love between the Father and the Son, so it naturally follows that the source of the Holy Spirit would be both of them. Augustine in his book *On The Trinity* is interested in the internal relationships of the three persons as one God, so that when God relates to the world it is in one unified action. Thus in

---

[9] Augustine, "On the Trinity," *NPNF* 3:227.

[10] Augustine, *The Trinity* 167.

[11] J. N. D. Kelly, *Early Christian Doctrines* (San Francisco: Harper & Row, 1960) 359.

regard to salvation God as a unity elects those predestined for salvation. The second person of the Trinity contributes his death as a sacrifice for sin, which makes election possible. However, since the election occurred before the foundation of the world, before the incarnation in Jesus, and before the fall of Adam and Eve, the relationship or dependence of salvation upon the event of the incarnation is questionable. It seems in fact that the salvation of humanity is dependent solely upon the election of God apart from God's life as Trinity.

The description of salvation as predestination removes any necessity for God to be Trinity in order to bring about the salvation of the world. Thus God as Trinity has been separated from the God of salvation who is one and omnipotent, all powerful. The Trinity will continue to function in Western Christian theology, but it will be primarily an organizing structure for Christian education. It is no longer the central doctrine that is necessary in order to describe how God is related to the world in a way that necessarily brings about salvation.

Martin Luther

Luther describes salvation in terms of justification. Human beings are justified by grace through faith. This was his discovery made while reading Paul's letter to the Romans. Since he, like Augustine, was convinced that he could never possibly do "enough" to become acceptable to God, it was critical for Luther to find a gracious God who would do everything necessary to bring about salvation. This need arose from Luther's assessment of the human condition about which he says, "For in us and from us grows nothing but unholiness and uncleanness. Whether I become a barefoot friar or a monk and work-righteous person of a different order, I remain a condemned sinner just as I was born from Adam."[12]

Luther adopts the doctrine of original sin from the Roman Catholic tradition. The Lutheran Church's support for this doctrine is clearly stated in the Augsburg Confession, Article II, "This inborn sickness and hereditary sin is truly sin and condemns to the eternal wrath of God all those who are not born again through Baptism and the Holy Spirit."[13]

Thus the grace of God that is required for salvation comes to us from outside ourselves. Since we have nothing to contribute, this guarantees that salvation is clearly an act of God for us. Luther was convinced by ob-

---

[12] *Luther's Works,* ed. Jaroslav Pelikan (Philadelphia: Fortress, 1973) 24:170.

[13] *The Book of Concord: The Confessions of the Evangelical Lutheran Church,* ed. and trans. by Theodore G. Tappert, in collaboration with Jaroslav Pelikan, Robert H. Fischer, Arthur C. Piepkorn (Philadelphia: Fortress, 1959) 29.

serving his parishioners and the people in his town that we remain sinners all our lives even though we have been baptized. He was most disappointed that he could not tell the baptized from the unbaptized in his own community. This did raise the question for him of why some people have faith and others do not. He answered this by recognizing that this is God's choice. Some are elected to salvation and necessarily others are not. This hidden God who operates throughout the world and causes all that happens is finally the one who determines salvation by giving the gift of faith to some and not to others. The Lutheran Confessions describe the concept of the eternal election of God as "a useful, salutary, and comforting doctrine, for it mightily substantiates the article that we are justified and saved without our works and merit, purely by grace and solely for Christ's sake" (SD XI, 43).[14] This salvation is something that actually occurs only after death. Our life continues to be unholy and unclean, but God has promised to see us as clean and holy even though we are not. This is described as the "cheerful exchange." Christ takes on our sin and we take on his righteousness. Therefore we are *simul justus, simul peccator,* that is, at the same time justified, at the same time a sinner. But nothing concrete necessarily occurs. Thus there is no expectation for change or growth in grace; rather, any actualization of this reestablished relationship between God and humanity will await death. Justification means that we, the ungodly, are objectively declared righteous by God even though there is no evidence of that imputed righteousness until death. The role of faith is to underscore that this justification is "for me." This realization frees me from focusing attention on doing enough to earn my salvation and frees me to serve my neighbor who has needs.

That this salvation of humanity is possible is due to the work of Christ. Luther follows the Western tradition after Anselm in describing the work of Christ in terms of sacrifice and satisfaction: "the incarnation and death of Jesus Christ proclaim that God gives up his sinless Son and punishes him in order that the sinner might go unpunished and live."[15] The Augsburg Confession, Article III, says that the purpose of the life and death of Jesus is "in order to be a sacrifice not only for original sin but also for all other sins and to propitiate God's wrath."[16] For humanity this means that Jesus has suffered for the sins of humanity so that our sins are forgiven by God and we become holy in God's sight. This is the "cheerful exchange" understanding of how the work of Christ justifies sinners.

---

[14] Edmund Schlink, *Theology of the Lutheran Confessions,* tr. Paul F. Koehneke and Herbert J. A. Bouman (Philadelphia: Fortress, 1961) 295.

[15] Schlink, *Confessions* 84.

[16] *Book of Concord* 30.

Edmund Schlink argues that the doctrine of the Trinity is "the basis of the Lutheran Confessions and it determines the structure of all their doctrinal statements."[17] However, Schlink also recognizes that while it provides structure it is not the central, integrating doctrine of the whole of the theology, since he also comments, "nevertheless, in the Confessions the doctrine of the Trinity is evidently quoted as a presupposition rather than developed and proved dogmatically. After all it is taken over as a finished and settled doctrine."[18] Luther and Lutheran doctrine have accepted the doctrine of the Trinity, as Augustine did, as a completed work that no longer requires integration into a theological construction rather different from the theology that gave rise to the Eastern Trinity. Luther follows Augustine in saying "that the three 'persons' cannot be theologically distinguished from each other by anything else than their respective relationships to one another as Father, Son and Spirit."[19] This description does not relate the doctrine of the Trinity to the understanding of salvation developed by Luther or to the christology he inherited. Eric Gritsch wants to link the Trinity with Luther's understanding of salvation and claims that "the dogma of the Trinity proclaims that God was incarnate in Christ 'for me' *(pro me),* that is, for the sake of my salvation."[20] While this links God (Father?) with Christ, it in no way provides any clue as to the role of the Holy Spirit. This can undergird God as diad but not God as Trinity. This christocentric focus will be encountered in most Protestant theologians, including John Calvin. The tendency in Protestant theology is to accept the Trinity as a doctrine of the Church and to use it to organize confessions and catechisms, but to ignore its original function as the doctrine that integrates other primary doctrines, i.e., Christology and soteriology and the doctrine of God. It is curious that the discussion of Luther's theology by Paul Althaus devotes twenty-five pages to God without mentioning the Trinity, and that the Trinity receives all of two pages beginning on p. 199. This discussion is indicative of the priorities in Luther's theology. Clearly the Trinity functions not as the integrating element for the theology, but on the periphery.

John Calvin

Calvin, like Luther and Augustine, distinguishes between those who have been elected by God for salvation and those who have not. Calvin is

[17]   Schlink, *Confessions* 65.

[18]   Ibid. 66.

[19]   Paul Althaus, *The Theology of Martin Luther,* tr. Robert C. Schultz (Philadelphia: Fortress, 1981) 200.

[20]   Eric W. Gritsch, *Martin—God's Court Jester* (Philadelphia: Fortress, 1983) 107.

more forthright in acknowledging that in effect when some are elected the rest are condemned. He insists that he is complying with Scripture when he writes in *The Institutes* "that by an eternal and immutable counsel, God has once for all determined, both whom he would admit to salvation and whom he would condemn to destruction" (III. xxi. 7).[21]

This eternal election is based on God's mercy and is necessary because we can do nothing to merit or contribute to our own salvation. It is necessary that we not be required to contribute anything, because Calvin's assessment of human nature is basically negative. Calvin follows Augustine in defining original sin as "the depravation of a nature previously good and pure" (II. i. 5).[22] The divine image of God in which we were created is obliterated in Adam and so lost for all of humanity. What we inherit from Adam is an "innate depravity" so that "even before we behold the light of life, we are in the sight of God defiled and polluted."[23] Clearly it is necessary for God to effect salvation on behalf of humanity, since humans are incapable of doing anything that is good apart from God.

Calvin follows Luther in placing the reality of salvation after death, "where the elect are resurrected in their same bodies but with a different quality" (III. xxv. 8).[24] There is no expectation of salvation on earth, or that it might include more than humanity, or that humanity might participate in sanctification before death. Calvin speaks of this world negatively. He writes that "we should habituate ourselves to a contempt of the present life, that we may thereby be excited to meditation on that which is to come" (III. ix. 1).[25] He further notes that "nothing can be sought or expected on earth but conflict" and he describes the "world as a sepulchre" and our "body as a prison" (III. ix. 4). What is available to the elect now is the Holy Spirit, who is a power external to them/us, who reveals to their/our minds and confirms in their/our hearts that God is gracious toward them/us. Again, as for Luther, faith is the assurance that God is "for us" so that we can live with confidence that God is gracious. We should not worry about salvation since it is God's work alone. We should concentrate on obeying God's commands and serving others.

In order for the elect to experience salvation it was necessary for Christ to die and rise again. Christ is a sacrifice that makes satisfaction for our sins to appease the wrath of God and also abolishes our guilt, which we received from Adam (II. xv. 6). This Anselmian interpretation of the work

---

[21] Hugh T. Kerr, *A Compend of The Institutes of the Christian Religion by John Calvin* (Philadelphia: Westminster, 1964) 129.

[22] Ibid. 43.

[23] Ibid.

[24] Ibid. 146.

[25] Ibid. 128.

of Christ influences the way the Nicene Creed is interpreted. Calvin argues that the reason Christ "descended into hell" was because it was necessary for him to "feel the severity of the divine vengeance, in order to appease the wrath of God, and satisfy his justice" (II. xvi. 10).[26] In contrast to this interpretation the Eastern Christian tradition interprets this phrase from the Creed to indicate that Christ retrieved all people back to Adam and Eve so that they might participate in salvation. Calvin's focus on the death of Christ to appease the wrath of God and his narrowing of salvation to the elect seem to account for this difference in interpretation.

For Calvin the death of Christ, as a sacrifice, seems more necessary to salvation than his resurrection. Calvin admits that "our salvation is perfectly accomplished by his death" (II. xv. 13).[27] This focus on Christ's death seems to occur along with the shift from death to sin as the problem for humanity. In the Eastern tradition sin is certainly an issue, but that all people die is the major problem. So the focus is on the resurrection in which Christ overcomes death and the grave, granting eternal life. Calvin also acknowledges the resurrection and that by it death is conquered, but the focus in the West has shifted to Christ's death on the cross. Even so Calvin says that the Christian's faith rests on the resurrection so that both the death and resurrection of Christ are required for salvation.

Calvin organizes his theology in *The Institutes of the Christian Religion* according to the Trinity. Book I is "God the Creator." Book II is "Jesus Christ the Redeemer." Book III is "The Holy Spirit," and Book IV is "The Holy Catholic Church." Actually the chapter on the Trinity is Chapter VI of Book I. Preceding this chapter are five chapters that discuss the knowledge of God apart from the Trinity. Only two chapters begin with a section titled "the doctrine stated." One is the chapter on the doctrine of election and the other is the chapter on the doctrine of the Trinity. Clearly Calvin considers both of these doctrines to be part of the received theology of the Church.

In stating the doctrine of the Trinity Calvin indicates that he is not ultimately interested in the contention over words that marked the discussions in the past. Instead he wants people to understand that "when the Scripture speaks of one God, it should be understood of a unity of substance; and that, when it speaks of three in one essence, it denotes the Persons in this Trinity" (I. xiii. 5).[28]

In explaining the doctrine of the Trinity Calvin relies on Augustine, who distinguishes between the substance which is one and the three who are

---

[26] Ibid. 83.

[27] Ibid.

[28] Ibid. 23.

described as reciprocal relations. Calvin also follows Augustine by indicating that "the Son is said to be from the Father, and the Spirit from both the Father and the Son" (I. xiii. 18).[29]

Conclusion

Augustine, Luther, and Calvin all received the doctrine of the Trinity as a settled doctrine of the Church that requires acknowledgment. Augustine's Trinity of divine simplicity in the one substance expressed in three Persons who are distinguished by their relationships is adopted by Luther and Calvin. It is this doctrine of the Trinity, which includes the simple substance and the double procession of the Holy Spirit, that Vladimir Lossky, an Eastern Christian theologian, argues makes salvation as *theosis* impossible. "After the Councils of Lyons and Florence . . . it became impossible for Roman Catholic theologians to admit the energetic manifestation of the Trinity as something not contradicting the truth of the divine simplicity. No longer was there any place for the concept of the energies of the Trinity: nothing was admitted to exist outside the divine essence except created effects, acts of will analogous to the act of creation. Western theologians had to profess the created character of glory and of sanctifying grace, to renounce the concept of deification; and in doing this they are quite consistent with the premises of their triadology."[30]

The difference in the understanding of the Trinity leads to a different way of describing salvation. Through the removal of the energies of God from the world and from human nature in particular the image of God in humanity is so overcome by sin as to be lost. Lossky locates the grace of God within us, and it is this grace that is the divine energies as they are communicated to and appropriated by human beings that makes salvation as deification possible. Once the image is lost and the grace of God becomes external to us *theosis* becomes impossible. What then develops is a doctrine of salvation that is objective. It happens to humanity without humanity's free assent or cooperation. The internal connection between God and humanity in human nature is no longer possible, nor is the direct experience of God by humans in a mystical experience possible.

The effects of salvation in the West are mediated by the assurance of faith rather than directly experienced as in the East. This is because the doctrine of salvation in the West is based on Augustine's doctrine of the Trinity and on Augustine's conviction that human beings are by nature sinful

---

[29] Ibid. 26.

[30] Vladimir Lossky, *In the Image and Likeness of God,* ed. John H. Erickson and Thomas E. Bird (New York: St. Vladimir's Seminary Press, 1974) 96.

and thus incapable of cooperating with or participating in salvation other than by being elected by God in spite of their sinfulness. Luther and Calvin both follow not only Augustine's doctrine of the Trinity but also his understanding of salvation as election and his assessment of humanity as most profoundly sinful even to the point of depravity according to Calvin. The understanding of the work of Christ in Luther and Calvin seems more indebted to Anselm, but it is not inconsistent with Augustine. For the Western theologians the focus of theology is Christ and his role in salvation. The notion of the Trinity as theology, which is the Eastern understanding, is lost, and the role of the Holy Spirit is now to bring faith rather than to make possible the transfiguration of humanity and, through humanity, of the whole world. These changes are at least not prevented by, and if Lossky is correct are actually made possible by the Western doctrine of the Trinity, which does not function as the central doctrine into which all other doctrines are integrated but functions alongside the doctrines of salvation and the work of Christ. The doctrine of salvation understood as election does not require a doctrine of God as Trinity.

Chapter Three

Recent Formulations of the Augustinian Tradition

Three recent theologians will be examined, all of whom have written about the Trinity. All are in the Western Christian tradition and remain influenced by Augustine. They have all formulated their ideas since 1945. They are Karl Barth, Eberhard Jüngel, and Robert Jenson. Both Jüngel and Jenson have been influenced by Barth, although Jenson is critical of both Augustine and Barth.

Karl Barth

Karl Barth was deeply influenced by the reality that many churches and Christian believers supported the Nazi regime during World War II. Although he lived in Basel, Switzerland, he was instrumental in bringing about the Confessing Church in Germany, which was opposed to Hitler. He was convinced that theology should be written in such a way that it would not be influenced by current events in the world. He achieved that goal. The first volume of his *Church Dogmatics* was published in Zurich in 1947 and includes his doctrine of the Trinity.

For Barth the doctrine of the Trinity is bound to his doctrine of revelation. "We come to the doctrine of the Trinity by no other way than by that of an analysis of the concept of revelation."[1] Conversely, "Revelation to be rightly interpreted must be interpreted as the ground of the doctrine of the Trinity."[2] Revelation is the act of God revealing himself as Lord. It is the

---

[1] Karl Barth, *Church Dogmatics I.1.* Chapter II, Part I, "The Triune God" (New York: Scribner, 1969) 358.

[2] Ibid. 359.

person of Jesus revealed as Lord that is the foundation of the Trinity. Barth is concerned to avoid any possible charge of tritheism, thus "three-in-oneness in God does not mean a three-fold deity, either in the sense of a plurality of deities or in the sense of the existence of a plurality of individuals or parts within the one deity. The name of Father, Son and Spirit means that God is the one God in threefold repetition."[3]

Since there is not a plurality at all there is complete identity of essence and therefore all three are necessarily equal. Further, Barth rejects the use of the term "person" lest it be construed to mean personality and lead to having three personalities in God. Rather he prefers to say "we are speaking not of three divine 'I's, but thrice of the one divine 'I'."[4] Barth wants to locate this Trinity between modalism which fails to distinguish among the three, and tritheism, which distinguishes so much among the three that the unity is lost. Barth therefore rejects two very different definitions of the term "person." First he rejects the definition of person that is associated with the Greek word *prosopon,* which is the mask worn by Greek actors and thus in Trinitarian thinking leads directly to modalism. The second and opposite meaning of person is the same as individual, i.e., separated, singular, and unrelated to anyone or anything else. This definition comes from Boethius by way of Thomas Aquinas to Barth. "Person is the singular rational individual essence."[5] Following this definition would require three essences in God, and Barth rejects that as well. It is also significant that Barth uses this definition of person because he has previously defined freedom in terms of "ontic and noetic independence."[6] For Barth God's revelation as Lord means that God must be free vis à vis everything. Nevertheless he believes that the members of the Trinity cannot be free in their interrelationships without tritheism. Since Barth is primarily concerned to uphold monotheism, his biggest fear is tritheism. To avoid this he bases his Trinity in revelation. Thus "it follows directly from the Trinitarian understanding of the God revealed in Scripture that this one God is to be regarded not only as an impersonal lordship, i.e. as power, but as the Lord, and so not only as absolute Spirit but as a Person, i.e. as an I existive in and for Itself with a thought and will proper to it."[7]

Barth continues by stating that he prefers the term "mode of being" to "person" for the aforementioned reasons. He thinks that "'individual mode of existence' should ever more clearly reveal itself, as the kernel of what

[3] Ibid. 402.
[4] Ibid. 403.
[5] Ibid. 409.
[6] Ibid. 352.
[7] Ibid. 412.

a dogmatics has to hold fast to of the old concept of Person."[8] The three "modes of being" in God are distinguishable in their separate manifestations but Barth insists that "this relatively distinct manifestation of the three modes of existence does not imply a corresponding state of distinctness among themselves."[9] They are distinct only in terms of their relations to each other. The Father is the Begetter who begets the Son, the Begotten, and the two of them together bring forth "a third thing common to both . . . which originates in common from Begetter and Begotten."[10] This he relates back to revelation by saying that "only because there is a veiling of God can there be an unveiling and only by there being a veiling and an unveiling of God can there be a self-impartation of God."[11] Here Barth is clearly following Augustine's example by claiming that the "third thing" comes from both the Father and the Son. Barth describes the relationship of these three modes of existence to each other: "where there is distinction, there is also community, a definite participation by each mode of existence in the other modes of existence."[12] This is intended to be the conventional notion of coinherence *(perichoresis)*. However, *perichoresis* originally assumes both actual distinctions and actual relations among the three. Barth makes it clear that such actual distinctions are not what he intends: "we must believe that those distinctions in the operations of God really take place within the sphere and limits of our conceivability, but that even here they neither properly nor primarily signify the last word in the hidden essence of God, that in these distinctions cannot rest the distinctions in God Himself."[13]

Thus for Barth monotheism, or the belief in God revealed as Lord, is clearly more important than God as Trinity. The fear of tritheism is so great that God as Trinity becomes a matter of our perception only and not an accurate description of God. Therefore God is actually one, and it is only in our limited ability to conceive that God becomes three. God as Trinity is subsumed under revelation so that, "it is God who reveals Himself in a like manner as the Father in His self-veiling and holiness, as He does as the Son in His self-unveiling and mercy, and as the Spirit in His self-impartation and love."[14] The one "I" is veiled, unveiled, and imparted. These are questionable distinctions that, as Barth says, do not qualify for the term person because the distinctions are not actual in God.

[8] Ibid. 415.
[9] Ibid.
[10] Ibid. 417.
[11] Ibid.
[12] Ibid. 418.
[13] Ibid. 427.
[14] Ibid. 438.

Again Barth follows Augustine in insisting on the primacy of the one. However, Barth goes beyond Augustine in denying actuality to the three. Augustine was describing God's own reality in his doctrine of the Trinity. For Barth the doctrine of the Trinity tells us nothing about God in God's self but it "tells us these two things, that He who reveals Himself according to Scripture, is to be feared and loved; to be feared because He can be God, and to be loved because He can be our God."[15] That "God reveals Himself as Lord"[16] is what is most important to Barth and he conforms his Trinity to fit his concept of revelation and maintain monotheism at the expense of making clear distinctions within the Trinity.

This monotheism as well as the concept of revelation fit well with Barth's understanding of christology and salvation. Jesus as Lord is the focus of Barth's theology. "Revelation culminates in the existence of Jesus of Nazareth."[17] He reveals God as the God of Israel and so Jesus is the fulfillment of the covenant God made with Abraham. The God who created the world (though he has no need of it) and Israel becomes a man in the existence of Jesus Christ and "is the *sovereign decision* upon the existence of everyman. A sovereign decision has been made about us men . . . the sovereign decision is imposed upon all men."[18]

Since this decision has been made, all people are claimed by God in Christ. In Jesus Christ everything about human beings has been decided. He takes on our sin, wickedness, misery, and death in his own act of humiliation. In this act we all become the property of God and are therefore bound to serve God. The reconciliation of sinful human beings to God in the life, death, and resurrection of Jesus Christ means that "God takes over the responsibility for us. We are now His property and He has the disposal of us. Our own unworthiness affects us no longer."[19] "We are no longer seriously regarded by God as sinners."[20] We remain sinful and unworthy from our perspective, but God has decided not to bring his wrath to bear on us since Jesus suffered by bearing the wrath of God for his whole life. This was necessary because to be human is to be placed before God and to deserve God's wrath. Thus in order to bring about reconciliation between God and humanity it was necessary for Jesus to be placed in the same situation as humanity and so to become the bearer of the wrath of God for us.

---

[15] Ibid. 440.
[16] Ibid. 431.
[17] Karl Barth, *Dogmatics in Outline* (New York: Harper & Row, 1959) 80.
[18] Ibid. 88.
[19] Ibid. 151.
[20] Ibid. 121.

It is in the Easter event that Jesus "begins a new life as the conqueror, as the victorious bearer, as the destroyer of the burden of man's sin, which had been laid upon Him."[21] The result of this event is that God's omnipotence and God's grace are now revealed to be the same thing. Also sin and death and all of world history have become past tense in Christ. He is the culmination of history, and what occurs after the Christ event is the anticipation of the Second Coming in which we will discover that the One who is to come is the One we already know in Jesus Christ. At his return the veil will be lifted and it will be obvious that what was needed has already occurred and that everything that happened was as it should have been. All our future will reveal to us is that "all was right and good in our existence and in this evil world-history and . . . in the still more evil Church history."[22]

Salvation and christology come together for Barth in establishing the objective fact that "Jesus has come and that He has spoken His word and done His work. That *exists* quite independently of whether we men believe it or not."[23] Those whom God elects are given the gift of the Holy Spirit, which brings people to faith and gathers them into congregations so that the word can be preached and so that they may wait for the Second Coming. The act of faith is the acceptance of one's situation in which God has decided to see each of us as a new creature rather than as the sinners that we really are. One's role as a human person is to be a witness to the mighty act of God in this decision of Jesus Christ. "The goal of creation, the object of the whole, the object of heaven and earth and all creation . . . is to be the theatre of His glory"[24] because this is where revelation occurs, culminating along with world history in Jesus Christ. There is no change in the world or in human persons since the focus is on God who is the only subject or actor in this production. Barth's Trinity operates in his christology where God is revealed a second time. Salvation is defined as election by God of the ungodly, which comes about by the revelation in Jesus Christ. Since for Barth "the whole work of God lives and moves in this one Person"[25] it is not possible or desirable for God to relate to the world apart from Jesus; hence the Trinity is reduced to one God who revealed Jesus to be Lord. This emphasis on Jesus, and therefore not on the other persons of the Trinity, has led in Western Christian theology to the Trinity becoming an abstract dogma that is no longer required to tell the story of salvation.

---

[21] Ibid. 122.
[22] Ibid. 134.
[23] Ibid. 132.
[24] Ibid. 58.
[25] Ibid. 39.

Barth has been treated first because he has been so influential in the development of recent Western doctrines of the Trinity. While those who follow do not necessarily agree completely with Barth, Jüngel and Jenson follow his and Augustine's pattern of beginning with the one and then scrambling to show how the three are distinct. All three also agree that God saves by election, so that the relationship between the Trinity and salvation as they describe it is very similar.

Eberhard Jüngel

Eberhard Jüngel is a German theologian following in Barth's footsteps. Thus he is consciously attempting to explicate Barth's thought. Indeed, Jüngel's work is based upon a sentence from Barth's *Church Dogmatics:* "Becoming should be understood ontologically, originally as a Trinitarian category, according to which God does not leave his present state behind him as a past in order to proceed towards a future which is unknown to him, but according to which he is in Trinitarian livingness 'undividedly the beginning, succession and end, all at once in his own essence.'" (*CD* II. I. 615).[26]

Jüngel supports Barth in claiming that the only way to avoid the hermeneutical problem of theology, that is, how to interpret the relationship of God to the world in this current time, is to ground theology in revelation alone. This, of course, requires "greater confidence in the capacity of revelation over reason."[27] Again, as for Barth, revelation is prior to Trinity. "Revelation as the self-interpretation of God is the root of the doctrine of the Trinity. Therefore the doctrine of the Trinity is the interpretation of revelation and therewith the interpretation of the being of God . . . ."[28]

Jüngel, like Barth, begins with the oneness of God but he proposes different language in seeking the distinctions. First there is "a whence of revelation," then "a becoming revealed which is grounded in this whence," and "a being revealed of God which is grounded in the whence and in the becoming revealed."[29] Although the language has changed the distinctions are still not clearly concrete and the third thing is also a product of the first two modes of being. Jüngel agrees with Barth that even while assigning different descriptions to the three modes of being "God assigns to himself his being as Father, as Son, as Spirit."[30]

---

[26] Eberhard Jüngel, *The Doctrine of the Trinity,* tr. Horton Harris (Edinburgh: Scottish Academic Press, 1976) viii.

[27] Ibid. 11.

[28] Ibid. 15.

[29] Ibid. 27.

[30] Ibid. 39.

Jüngel argues that "God's being as being is pure event,"[31] so that God's being is always in becoming in such a way that the distinctive modes are becoming together. "The modes of God's being which are differentiated from one another are so related to each other that each mode of God's being *becomes* what it *is* only together *with* the other two."[32] One wonders why both Barth and Jüngel pay such close attention to the relatedness of the three things when the distinctions have not been sufficiently con- cretized so as to make such attention necessary.

The oneness of God is maintained also in christology such that "the electing God in mode of being as Son and elected man Jesus are *one per- son* in Jesus Christ."[33] The mode of being as Son is differentiated from the Father by his obedience to the Father, which is not to be interpreted as sub- ordination. "The oneness of the Son of God and the Son of Man was fore- ordained from all eternity in the covenant God made with himself."[34] This is indicative of the fact that when Barth and Jüngel speak of God as rela- tional, they mean that God relates to one of the other modes of being in God. "The doctrine of the Trinity is an attempt to think out the self- relatedness of God's being."[35] This Trinity is not related to anything out- side itself, such as human beings or the world. This Trinity does not de- scribe God's relationship to the world, nor does it indicate that this relationship is significant for the world or for God. The Trinity is a closed system because what is most important is that "God corresponds to him- self" (*CD* II. I. 657 and 660). In actuality Barth's *Church Dogmatics* is ba- sically a detailed exegesis of this proposition.[36]

Jüngel also takes this criterion seriously. His delineation of Barth in his formulation of the Trinity is still dependent upon revelation and is used pri- marily to describe revelation. Jüngel has introduced the notion of becoming into the static idea of being in order to overcome the problem of time in God. Thus God now is an event and no longer a thing and God is clearly one, with the trinitarian distinctions, following Barth, rather unclear.

Robert Jenson

Robert Jenson is a contemporary Lutheran theologian in the United States. He places himself in the Western tradition by responding to Augustine and to Barth. He discards Augustine's notion of divine simplicity

[31] Ibid. 27.
[32] Ibid. 73.
[33] Ibid. 68.
[34] Ibid. 75.
[35] Ibid. 99.
[36] Ibid. 24.

and is critical of his separation of the doctrine of the Trinity from salvation history. Jenson understands that the problem created by this separation is the loss of the Trinity's original function. In response to Barth, Robert Jenson has expanded upon his development of the Trinity and taken the notion of time within God to its logical conclusion. While Jenson has stated the problem correctly, his reliance on Barth and his definition of time as eschatological make his solution inadequate.

Jenson begins by using Barth's structure of the Trinity as God in repetition. He also begins with revelation, and the sentence he exegetes is "God is the one who raised Israel's Jesus from the dead."[37] Jenson, like Barth, rejects the concept of person and offers in its place "identity." To have "three identities in God means three discrete sets of names and descriptions, each sufficient to specify uniquely, yet all identifying the same reality."[38]

Jenson considers "identity" preferable to "person" because "something's identity is the possibility of picking it out from the maelstrom of actuality, so as to talk about it,"[39] "to identify something is to pick it out *as* something *otherwise* known. Only that has identity which is repeatedly identifiable,"[40] and "'Identity' is now regularly used to interpret personal existence . . . it names the mode of repeated identifiability proper to certain entities, those we currently call 'personal' in a sense."[41] Therefore Jenson concludes "that there is even one identity of God means that God is personal, that he is God in that he does Godhead, in that he chooses himself as God."[42]

Jenson even uses Barth's vocabulary of repetition, event, and decision, which makes his indebtedness to this theologian all the more evident. "That there are three identities in God means that this God's deed of being the one God is three times repeated, and so that each repetition is a being of God, and so that only in this precise self-repetition is God the particular God that he in fact is. God does God, and over again, and yet over again—and only so does the event and decision that is this God occur."[43]

So for Jenson the trinitarian formula is "there is one event, God, of three identities."[44] In developing this, his own understanding of the Trinity,

---

[37] Robert Jenson, *The Triune Identity: God according to the Gospel* (Philadelphia: Fortress, 1982) 21.

[38] Ibid. 109.

[39] Ibid. 108.

[40] Ibid. 109.

[41] Ibid. 110.

[42] Ibid.

[43] Ibid. 111.

[44] Ibid. 114.

Jenson moves away from Barth. Jenson is most critical of Augustine because it was he who "experienced the triune character of God as one thing and the history of salvation as quite another. Thus the trinitarian formulas lost their original function."[45] It was also he who defined God in terms of Being itself, which led to "the most immediately destructive consequence . . . that God is 'simple' in a rigid sense that comes very close to the Arian refusal of all differentiation in God."[46] Jenson contends that at this point Augustine's thought is incompatible with the trinitarian theology of the Nicene Creed because "when the Nicenes called the Trinity as such God, they so named him *because* of the triune relations and differences; when Augustine calls the Trinity as such God, it is *in spite of* them."[47]

In Jenson's opinion it is necessary to discard Augustine's doctrine of divine simplicity in order to continue developing a viable understanding of the Trinity. The major problem created by this "divine simplicity" is the development in Western trinitarian thought of the notion of two Trinities, one "immanent" and one "economic." The "immanent Trinity" is God in relation to God's self. The "economic Trinity" is God in relation to the world. Jenson sees this as a problem in relating God to time. The "economic Trinity" is derived from observing God working in the world, in the past and in the present, and anticipating God's actions in the future. The "immanent Trinity" is clearly not time-bound and thus the problem of how to put the two together and maintain the freedom of God arises. In Western trinitarian thought, which will not let the relations be temporal, that God is described as "'one and three' becomes the mystification of western churchgoers . . . ."[48]

Thus it is not only necessary to discard "divine simplicity" but also to "free trinitarian doctrine from captivity to antecedent interpretation of deity as timelessness."[49] Once that is done it is possible to reconcile the two trinities, but "only if the identity of the 'economic' and 'immanent' Trinity is eschatological, if the 'immanent' Trinity is simply the eschatological reality of the 'economic.'"[50] Eschatological is used here to mean "at some time in the far distant future" or "at the end of time when Christ will come again." Jenson discards all notions of Christ prior to the birth of Jesus in Bethlehem and all notions of the Spirit prior to the sending of the Spirit to the apostles of the early church at Pentecost (Acts 2). God develops in time, one piece at a time, and only comes together as Trinity at the end

---

[45] Ibid. 115.

[46] Ibid. 118.

[47] Ibid. 119. (*Trin.* VII.2)

[48] Ibid. 125.

[49] Ibid. 138.

[50] Ibid. 139.

of time. The second person of the Trinity is not the Christ, but the man Jesus. "Truly, the Trinity is simply the Father and the man Jesus and their Spirit as the Spirit of the believing community."[51] Jenson sees this Trinity as recovering the original function of the doctrine by relating the Trinity to how God acts in a saving way in the world. This Trinity is also related to time in God, so that the three relate to past, present and future. Jenson is satisfied with this formulation because for him it meets Barth's criterion for truth in theology, namely, that God's freedom must be maintained (*CD* II/2, 155). "As for God's freedom, only this proposal fully asserts it. Genuine freedom is the reality of possibility, is openness to the future; genuine freedom is Spirit."[52] Spirit is for Jenson related to future so that the Spirit is defined as the "Power of the Eschaton."[53] While he also describes the Spirit as the Spirit of the believing community, he does not address how it is that this Power of the Eschaton relates to the believing community now.

Freedom here still keeps God separate from the world except in the event of Jesus. If the second person of the Trinity is the man Jesus that may indeed solve the problem of the pre-existent Christ, but it does very little to enhance our understanding of the Incarnation. Again Jenson does not address the "how" question in relation to the presence of God in Jesus. Since Jenson is following Barth, for whom the function of the doctrine of the Trinity is to identify God, there is apparently no impact on the world so far as salvation is concerned. The world is only a theater in which God acts in Jesus. Although Jenson has introduced the notion of time in God against Augustine's simplicity, his understanding of time as eschatological prevents it from being either cyclical or linear. Since this time points to a future event current happenings are devalued, and no real change can occur either in the world or in God. It is difficult to value God as event when time is only future and current events are of no consequence.

Conclusion

For these theologians the Trinity is a received doctrine that needs explaining but whose history has been lost. Thus Barth and Jüngel are most concerned about how the Trinity is really one and not three. This connection between God and the world is reserved for christology since it is only in Jesus as the Christ that God relates to the world, and then by means of election. The Father and Spirit are not related to the world except through Jesus. The Trinity does not exist in the world nor does it exist in God's self since this would compromise the oneness of God's essence.

[51] Ibid. 140.
[52] Ibid. 141.
[53] Ibid. 169.

Jenson moves away from Augustine's focus on the One and criticizes the divine simplicity of Augustine as well as his separation of the Trinity from salvation history. Jenson has diagnosed the problem correctly, but his solution is inadequate because of his indebtedness to Barth. While he joins the Trinity to salvation history, overcoming his perceived problem, he separates salvation history from the salvation of the world. Thus he focuses on an eschatological future that is where God will finally be Trinity and where salvation will finally occur.

Jenson, Jüngel, and Barth in an effort to remove theology from the context of the world have limited the salvific action of God in the world to Jesus and then only to the elect. God in Christ no longer permeates the world and the Spirit no longer transfigures the world into the kingdom of God by means of the work of the faithful. Instead, God makes a sovereign decision to forgive rather than punish, and this is revealed in Jesus who is the only instance of the presence of God in the world. And since salvation occurs in God and not in the world the role of the Holy Spirit is not to transfigure anything in this world, but to witness to the fact that Jesus is Lord. The difference in the understanding of salvation in East and West leads to a difference in the construction of the Trinity and to the limitation of the results of the work of Christ and the Spirit in the world.

These results were noted by Leonard Hodgson and Henry P. Van Dusen, who were concerned to revive the role of the Holy Spirit in order to better understand the Trinity, and by Cyril Richardson, who is convinced that the primary distinction is between God who is transcendent and God who is immanent and argues that the Trinity is not needed at all. These three theologians will be considered in the next chapter.

Chapter Four

Non-Augustinian Formulations in the Western Tradition

For most liberal Protestants the doctrine of the Trinity had been ignored because it was considered inauthentic, unimportant, or both. In an effort to recover authenticity a few thinkers broke with the Western tradition, including those to be discussed in this chapter: Leonard Hodgson, Henry P. Van Dusen, and Cyril Richardson.

For these three theologians the chief problem with the Western tradition is that it continues inauthentically to affirm the doctrine of the Trinity when its theology can only support two aspects and so is binitarian. They respond to this in opposite ways. Richardson accepts the binitarian theology and rejects the dogma of the Trinity. Hodgson and Van Dusen undertake to recover an authentic doctrine of the Holy Spirit as a divine Person and so to retain an authentically trinitarian doctrine of God.

Leonard Hodgson

Leonard Hodgson is critical of the Western tradition precisely because the Spirit has been lost as a distinct person in the Trinity and functions only as the relationship between the Father and the Son. This is true of the theologians discussed in the previous chapter because they base their work on Augustine, who was the first theologian to define the Spirit as a relationship. Hodgson wishes to recover a more social Trinity and take the distinctions between the persons seriously. He argues for a distinct role for the Spirit and redefines unity in a way that can account for the distinctness of the three without compromising the unity of God. But because he does

49

not relate the doctrine of the Trinity to the saving relationship of God to the world his Trinity remains an abstraction.

Hodgson's social trinity begins with the three persons; he attempts to show how the three are also one. Hodgson was accused by Western theologians of tritheism, which has consistently been the West's response to Trinitarian theology that proceeds in this manner.[1] Hodgson proposes a definition of unity based not on mathematics but on an organic model in which "approximation to the ideal is measured by a scale of intensity of unifying power."[2] Hodgson is updating the Patristic notion of *perichoresis* (coinherence) by insisting that "there are three elements perfectly unified in the Divine Life, and each of these elements is a Person. It is the main thesis . . . that the act of faith required for acceptance of the doctrine of the Trinity is faith in this unification, faith that the Divine unity is a dynamic unity actively unifying in the One Divine life the lives of the three Divine persons."[3] Hodgson is here intentionally beginning with the revelation of God in the Trinity, and he refuses to subordinate this revelation to the philosophical idea of oneness, i.e., undifferentiated simplicity. He thinks this is appropriate since in the patristic age "the views which came ultimately to be rejected as heretical were those which surrendered the revelation to the idea of unity."[4] This statement is true prior to Augustine, but as the hostile reception Hodgson's work received demonstrates, in the Western Christian tradition unity as undifferentiated simplicity has been the norm.

Hodgson argues that for contemporary theologians "to be true successors of the classical theologians, we must try to think as honestly in the terms of the thought of to-day"[5] as other theologians of the Church have done in the past. He locates the problem of the Trinity in the presupposed mathematical type of unity that is simplicity or oneness. He has discovered the scientific notion of "internal constitutive unities," which he believes God has contributed to this conversation. Thus following his predecessors he employs this "new" definition of unity as his contribution to understanding the revelation of God in the Trinity. For Hodgson, God as Trinity is revealed in the acts of God in history, and Hodgson speaks of these as empirical evidence of the Trinity. The Trinity functions for Hodgson as a formula for Christian living. Christians are to seek, find, and do "the Father's

---

[1] Note the third- and fourth-century controversies between East and West described in Chapter One.

[2] Leonard Hodgson, *The Doctrine of the Trinity* (New York: Charles Scribner's Sons, 1944) 93.

[3] Ibid. 95.

[4] Ibid. 99.

[5] Ibid. 175.

will in the Father's world with the companionship of the Son and by the guidance and strength of the Spirit."[6]

Hodgson deserves credit for being willing to update the discussion in his own tradition based on what he considered new scientific evidence. He was concerned to recover the "person" of the Holy Spirit that had become the "love between the Father and the Son" since Augustine. Therefore he emphasized the three persons and then sought their unity. He also used an organic understanding of unity rather than a mathematical definition to overcome the primary problem as he saw it: how to define "unity" so as to make the unity of the Trinity possible. Even though he began his Trinity in the Eastern manner with the revelation of God in three persons he was still trying to explain an abstract doctrine of God. He tried to make this God concrete by indicating that the Trinity is the pattern for Christian living. This does not, however, integrate christology, soteriology, and God in a way that describes how God's relationship to the world is one that saves the world.

Henry P. Van Dusen

Van Dusen, like Hodgson, attempts to recover the doctrine of the Trinity by focusing on the Holy Spirit. He does so by tracing the development of the doctrine of the Holy Spirit through the centuries. Finally, in his last chapter, he develops a doctrine of the Trinity. He argues that trinitarian speculation has taken one of two forms. It is either an "analogy from men's relations with each other to relations within the Divine Being"[7] or it is an "analogy from individual human consciousness to the inmost character of the Divine consciousness, justified by the basic recognition that 'man is made in the image of God.'"[8]

Van Dusen rejects both of these options in favor of a third, which he develops by applying the method of analogy. "It is the analogy of an individual human person in three aspects of his self-expression, in three functions and sets of relationships."[9] He uses Theodore Roosevelt as his example so that three different experiences of Roosevelt, as "forbidding statesman," as "rough plainsman," and as "gentle, boyish playmate" yield three different Roosevelts: "not 'three persons,' but one person in three separate 'modes of operation.'"[10] This doctrine of the Trinity is clearly modalistic since the

---

[6] Ibid. 178.

[7] Henry P. Van Dusen, *Spirit, Son and Father* (New York: Charles Scribner's Sons, 1958) 170.

[8] Ibid. 171.

[9] Ibid. 173.

[10] Ibid. 174.

distinctions are merely of different roles that one person plays during a lifetime. Van Dusen's recovery of the Holy Spirit does not sufficiently clarify the distinctions between the persons to avoid modalism.

Cyril Richardson

The final theologian to be considered here responded to the inauthenticity of the doctrine of the Trinity by rejecting it outright. Cyril Richardson refuses any attempt to configure God as Trinity because the Spirit is unnecessary to his understanding of God. Since the Trinity has become an abstract proposition and is divorced from the story of salvation his critique is justified. For Richardson God exists as transcendent (over and above the world) and immanent (in, with, and under the world) and any attempt to overcome or confuse this paradox is to compromise God; thus his critical attitude.

Richardson considers the Trinity to be an artificial construct that confuses paradoxes and contradictions in God that should be left to stand. He admits to distinctions within the Godhead but thinks the pattern of three is too simple and neat. His critique is valuable in that he recognizes that the Trinity is an attempt "to find appropriate language and symbols by which to express faith in the God who revealed himself in Jesus Christ,"[11] and also that "the fundamental difference is between the Father and the Son."[12] For Richardson these two represent the paradox that God is both transcendent and immanent. He objects to the Father-Son language because it destroys an equal paradox by assuming that the immanence is derived from the transcendence, that is, the Son is derived from the Father. He also is dissatisfied with Barth's terminology of God as veiled and God as unveiled. Thus Richardson concludes that "Barth's assumption that God by his nature cannot be unveiled to man and therefore must become 'God a second time' is unwarranted."[13] Richardson is, of course, operating with his own set of assumptions, namely that God is "self-sufficient and simple"[14] and that "the paradox can never be overcome and the very attempt to do so can only prove artificial."[15]

He considers the paradox to be compromised in the Church Fathers (he does not specify exactly who he means) who insist that the Father is the *archē,* the source of the Son and the Spirit, because this assumes that God

---

[11] Cyril Richardson, *The Doctrine of the Trinity* (Nashville: Abingdon, 1967) 15.
[12] Ibid. 19.
[13] Ibid. 36.
[14] Ibid. 38.
[15] Ibid. 38.

in his relations with the world is secondary to his essential being. He objects to the idea that the visible or revealed God can be derived from the invisible, self-sufficient, transcendent nature, because the transcendence is compromised in that event. Therefore "Barth's contention of the derivation of God's revealed mode of being from his hidden mode of being is open to the same objections."[16] He also criticizes Barth for treating "Father" exclusively under the term of "creator" because in so doing Barth has compromised his "veiled-unveiled" distinction.

Richardson denies any role for a third person, term, or thing by insisting that "if one sets up the primary distinction in terms of beyondness and relatedness, of veiling and unveiling, no third term is necessary. There is an antinomy, a paradox—no more."[17] Richardson thus criticizes the Western doctrines of the Trinity because of the insistence upon including the Spirit or third term. He points out that, following Augustine, the role of the Spirit in Western Trinities is to be the love or link between the Father and the Son. Thus the "Father and Son in [Western] Christian art are frequently personified, but not the Spirit. He is symbolized by the dove or the rays descending from the Father; but personal pictures of the Spirit have been comparatively rare and, indeed, have been finally condemned."[18]

Richardson shows that he is limiting himself to Western conceptualities by ignoring the fact that the icon of the Holy Trinity in Eastern Christian art is always a picture of the three angels—not men—who visit Abraham in Genesis 18. The Spirit, in icons of the Holy Trinity, is never represented as a dove but always as an angel. This is to indicate that these criticisms that Richardson is leveling against Western Christian doctrines of the Trinity do not apply to the Eastern Christian doctrine.

Richardson again takes issue with Barth for distinguishing the Son from the Spirit by speaking of the work of the Son as God's "self-revealing" and that of the Spirit as God's "self-imparting." "The difference between God's self-imparting and his self-revealing is not a difference which leads us to distinguish two separate persons in the Trinity."[19]

Richardson considers the trinities proposed by Sabellius and by Friedrich Schleiermacher, a nineteenth-century German theologian, "unsatisfactory because they are based upon experience, therefore can only speak of God revealed,"[20] i.e., there is no absolute "beyond" dimension, so that the

[16] Ibid. 67.

[17] Ibid. 69.

[18] Ibid. 101. The personification of the Spirit was condemned by Pope Benedict XIV in the eighteenth century.

[19] Ibid. 109.

[20] Ibid. 124.

transcendence of God is compromised and the transcendent-immanent paradox is not upheld.

Richardson's only comments about an Eastern Christian theologian are aimed at proving that the Trinity cannot be established by an analysis of God's activity in the world.[21] He objects to Gregory of Nyssa's description of the Father as the Source, the Son as the actualization in the world, and the Spirit as the transfigurer of persons and the world because this description does not account for God as Absolute. "The real paradox of God as both absolute and related has been transferred to the divine essence. The distinction between the Father and Son thus becomes unnecessary."[22] Richardson thus ignores the Eastern view that the Trinity describes how God's relationship to the world is salvific. With this understanding all three persons are indeed necessary.

Richardson is somewhat correct in that the paradox of absoluteness and relatedness in Eastern Christian theology is dealt with in terms of the distinction between the essence of God and the energies of God.[23] The persons of the Trinity then are among the energies of God, since God as Trinity is known. The transcendence of God is protected by the unknowableness of the essence of God. The distinction between the Father and the Son is that the Son becomes incarnate in the person of Jesus Christ and the Father does not. This is a rather different theological system that grants more value to the experience of God in the Church and in the world and considers this experience to be a primary source for doing theology. Richardson finds this to be unsatisfactory because it can only comment on the revealed God. The East assumes that God has integrity so that God revealed in God's energies is consistent with God's essence, although that essence is so extensive that it cannot be known, nor can it be adequately expressed in language. What God reveals is God, so that God is revealed as Trinity because that is who God is, that is how God relates in a saving way to the world, and that is how the Church throughout the ages has experienced God.

For Richardson the terms of the Trinity are merely "ways of thinking about God from different points of view."[24] There are not three persons or *hypostases* but only the paradox of transcendence and immanence. Richardson considers the transcendent and immanent characteristics fundamental to God, but not the notion of Trinity. The only helpful persons would be the Father who is transcendent and the Son who is immanent. The Spirit is unnecessary.

---

[21] Ibid. 140.

[22] Ibid. 135.

[23] This distinction is original to Gregory Nazianzus (*Or.* 38.7) and is further developed by Gregory Palamas *(The Triads)*.

[24] Richardson, *Trinity* 46.

Richardson criticizes one other Western theologian: Leonard Hodgson. Richardson objects to Hodgson's social doctrine of the Trinity because he considers it to be tritheistic. Thus he states, "if there are three centers of consciousness in God, there are three Gods. . . . It is simply impossible to say that God is really one in some ultimate sense, and still retain the idea of distinct centers of consciousness, which stand over against each other."[25] Richardson's other objection to Hodgson is that he sees no reason to continue using the traditional Father-Son language, since Richardson thinks that this language implies that the Father is somehow more God than the Son.[26] This could be more of a problem for Richardson than others, especially since Hodgson argues against the "monarchy" of the Father. He states that "in this unity there is no room for any trace of subordinationism, and that the thought of the Father as the Source or Fount of Godhead is a relic of pre-Christian theology which has not fully assimilated the Christian revelation."[27] Today we might criticize Hodgson's use of Father-Son language and wish that he had developed something else. Yet, considering the reaction Hodgson received using conventional language, imagine his rejection had he also proposed new language for the Trinity in 1944! Given Hodgson's context and his claim to base his Trinity upon the revelation of God as Trinity, the terminology Father, Son, Spirit is probably included in the revelation. (Jenson thought so in 1986.) In any case this was not a particular issue for Hodgson, even though it may be for Richardson.

Conclusion

None of these twentieth-century doctrines of the Trinity escapes the limitations imposed on Western trinitarian thought by Augustine. In none of them does the Trinity function as in the East to integrate christology, soteriology, and God. Richardson has decided against explaining the Trinity. Instead he insists that the Trinity is not necessary because there is no role for the Spirit to play. God is revealed as paradox, being both transcendent and immanent at the same time. Richardson's reaction against the Western tradition of Trinity as abstract and confusing is helpful in clarifying the problem.

Hodgson and Van Dusen want to recover the Holy Spirit as a distinct person since this Trinity is based on the revelation in the Scriptures. They consider the sending of the Spirit to be one of the acts of God, and that this

---

[25] Richardson, *Trinity* 94.

[26] Ibid.

[27] Hodgson, *Doctrine* 102.

reveals God to be Trinity. The problem they then faced was: how is this Trinity a unity if the Spirit no longer performs the unifying function, as it had for Augustine and subsequent Western theologians? Hodgson solves this problem by applying a new definition of unity that relies on the intensity of the relationships and not on a mathematical understanding of unity as oneness. Van Dusen solves this problem by using an analogy that is modalistic. The function of Hodgson's Trinity is to be a pattern for Christian living. Although Hodgson recovers some of the original meaning of the Trinity, neither he nor Van Dusen develops a Trinity that functions to integrate christology, soteriology, and a doctrine of God in a coherent manner. In these cases, as in the other Western doctrines thus far considered, the Trinity functions as an abstract doctrine that requires explanation. The clear exception is Richardson, for whom the doctrine of the Trinity does not function at all. Hence, in the West, the Trinity is no longer the core doctrine around which theology revolves.

Chapter Five

The Doctrine of the Trinity by Jürgen Moltmann

This chapter examines the work of a current Western theologian who has been influenced by Eastern Orthodox Christian theology and whose concern is to develop theology around a doctrine of the Trinity.

Jürgen Moltmann is a German theologian who is arguing for a Trinitarian doctrine of God against theologians who argue for a monotheistic conception of God. He rejects much of the Western Christian tradition in which he was trained and has learned from the Eastern Christian tradition, the tradition of Athanasius, in formulating his doctrine of the Trinity. He understands the integrative function of the Trinity and thus provides a model of how an authentic Western doctrine of the Trinity should be formulated. He is developing a historical and social doctrine of the Trinity based upon the history of Jesus and he is also concerned to show the correspondence between the relationships in the Trinity and the relationships of people to God, to other people, and to the world. Since for Moltmann "All theological statements which the Christian faith makes about God . . . have to be understood and interpreted as the expression of Christian moral existence"[1] the correspondence between God and the world is absolutely necessary to this doctrine of the Trinity.

Moltmann is critical of those who follow Augustine in what Moltmann terms a "monotheistic conception of the doctrine of the Trinity."[2] Barth is a good example. The object of the doctrine of God is to establish God's sovereignty or lordship. Therefore the doctrine of the Trinity must also

---

[1] Jürgen Moltmann, *The Trinity and the Kingdom,* tr. Margaret Kohl (San Francisco: Harper & Row, 1981) 62.

[2] Ibid. 63.

uphold this sovereignty and does so by locating the unity of the Trinity in the unified lordship of God. This seems to Moltmann to establish one divine subject and reduces the "three persons" to three "modes of being." Indeed, this is Barth's own vocabulary. Moltmann considers this to be unacceptable because it does not acknowledge the distinct existence of the three persons of the Trinity.

The Trinity Moltmann develops is based on salvation history. All three persons of the Trinity are necessary to this salvation history, which has its central focus in the cross. In this event and no other the Father surrenders the Son, who suffers and dies and is separated from the Father. However, the Spirit links them during this break in the relationship. "To put it in Trinitarian terms, the Father lets his Son sacrifice himself through the Spirit. The Cross is at the center of the Trinity."[3] It is in this relationship that the names for the Trinity are established. "Father" is part of the revelation in Jesus because he called God "Father." This name, Father, is only in relation to this Son, which again is not a title but a proper name.

The actual form of the Trinity varies as salvation history unfolds: Initially "the Father gives up his Son to death in its most absolute sense, for us. The Son gives himself up, for us. The common sacrifice of the Father and the Son comes about through the Holy Spirit, who joins and unites the Son in his forsakenness with the Father."[4] Next "the Father raises the Son through the Spirit; the Father reveals the Son through the Spirit; the Son is enthroned as Lord of God's kingdom through the Spirit."[5] Then "the Father raises the dead Son through the life-giving Spirit; the Father enthrones the Son, as Lord of his kingdom; the risen Son sends the creative Spirit from the Father to renew heaven and earth."[6]

However, this is not yet the end of the story. This history of salvation is completed only when the Son hands the kingdom over to the Father. This event brings about the kingdom of glory, which occurs in God's essential nature because God becomes all in all, and it also creates a new heaven and a new earth. Until this eschatological realization the salvation of the world remains provisional, so that only in the end "the Father subjects everything to the Son; the Son transfers the consummated kingdom to the Father; the Son subjects himself to the Father"[7] and the history of salvation is completed. Clearly this doctrine of the Trinity is closely tied to the history of salvation from the initial revelation in Jesus to the consummation of heaven and earth in the kingdom of glory.

---

[3] Ibid. 83.
[4] Ibid.
[5] Ibid. 88.
[6] Ibid. 89.
[7] Ibid. 92.

Moltmann insists that this Trinity is not only historical, but social as well. He locates the unity of this Trinity in the fellowship the three persons enjoy together. Thus he presents an italicized sentence that summarizes his approach: *"The New Testament talks about God by proclaiming in narrative the relationships of the Father, the Son, and the Spirit, which are relationships of fellowship and are open to the world."* [8] These relationships are non-hierarchical and provide the pattern upon which the relationships in the kingdom of God are based. "In this kingdom God is not the Lord; He is the merciful Father. In this kingdom there are no servants; there are only God's free children. In this kingdom what is required is not obedience and submission; it is love and free participation." [9]

Moltmann is intentionally redefining freedom. It is no longer to be understood as freedom over, i.e., the freedom to dispose of things and people. Rather freedom is freedom with, i.e., in relationship to others as equals. In God's relationship to the world this means that God provides space for humanity to exercise freedom and responsibility, thus limiting his power to insure free human interaction. It is in fellowship with the Son that people are "co-opted sons and daughters of the Father" [10] so that they may live in God and so that God may live in them. Freedom requires community; "the truth of freedom is love. . . . I become truly free when I open my life for other people and share with them . . . ." [11] This understanding of freedom as well as the realization that "it is a typically Western bias to suppose that social relationships and society are less 'primal' than the person" [12] are necessary in order to achieve a non-hierarchical unified Trinity.

Moltmann further emphasizes the unity of the persons of the Trinity by the use of the notion of *perichoresis*. By this term he means that the three persons live and exist in one another and also adds that "they also bring one another mutually to manifestation in the divine glory." [13] He considers this understanding sufficient to avoid any possibility of subordinating any one person to any other person in the Trinity as well as to achieve the unity of the three persons. *Perichoresis* in the Trinity corresponds to the experience of the Christian community which the Spirit unites. "The more open-mindedly people live with one another, for one another and in one another in the fellowship of the Spirit, the more they will become one with the Son and the Father, and one in the Son and the Father (John 17.21)." [14]

[8] Ibid. 64.
[9] Ibid. 70.
[10] Ibid. 122.
[11] Ibid. 216.
[12] Ibid. 199.
[13] Ibid. 176.
[14] Ibid. 158.

This union is also open to the world in a way that makes possible the uniting of the Trinity with creation and includes creation in itself. Again the Trinity is a description of salvation, not only for people but for all of creation. At the basis of this social Trinity is the concept of relationship. Moltmann begins by assuming that the relationship between God and the world is reciprocal because it is dynamic. It must be dynamic because God is a living God who desires to inhabit this creation. Therefore God influences the world, and in return the world influences God. God is continually creating the world by providing space within himself by limiting his power so that both freedom and chaos are possible in the world. Classical Western theology has included the world in creation but has not always included the whole world in salvation. Moltmann follows his Eastern Orthodox lead here and extends the scope of salvation to include the universe. Similarly he begins with creation rather than with the Fall because he includes time as a significant part of creation. This guarantees that change will be a necessary structure of the world, since "time is only perceived through change."[15]

He is also indebted to Orthodox theology for the image of salvation as transfiguration. This expectation views salvation as the gradual transformation of the world into God's own world so that God may dwell there in a way that is readily apparent to all. Because this has been the goal since the creation, the incarnation of the Son and the indwelling of the Spirit in believers are further steps along the road that leads to salvation. For Orthodox theology this process occurs in history, gradually manifesting the presence of God in the world. For Moltmann the transfiguration of the whole world awaits the indwelling of God in the universe. According to Moltmann's history of salvation this only occurs at the time of the kingdom of glory or at the end. Until that time this transfiguration apparently is "provisional."

Moltmann understands well that in this doctrine of the Trinity salvation and christology come together. For him the relationship of the Trinity to the world is by means of the Son as the Logos through whom God creates the world. The Son is also the image *(eikōn)* of the destiny of human persons. "In the incarnation of the Son the Triune God enters into the limited, finite situation. . . . He becomes the *human* God. . . . God's self-humiliation is completed and perfected in the passion and death of Jesus the Son."[16] The Son accepts and adopts being human and makes it part of his eternal life. Moltmann stresses the humiliation of God in adopting human nature, which he describes as threatened and perverted. While

[15] Ibid. 100.
[16] Ibid. 118.

Orthodox theology might speak of human nature as threatened, it is not "perverted." Here Moltmann is following Augustine and the notion of original sin, which presupposes a separation of nature and grace that is not part of an Orthodox understanding of the world or of humanity. This departure is also apparent when Moltmann speaks of the Son as the image of the destiny of humankind rather than of humanity being created in the image of God from the beginning. In Orthodox thought this image is never lost because while sin is understood to be prevalent in the world it is not part of human nature. This image for Orthodoxy is the starting point for transfiguration. Hence Moltmann's separation of nature and grace, while it may increase God's humiliation in becoming human, also calls into question the notion of salvation as transfiguration. For Moltmann humans are starting this transfiguration from a perverted, sinful nature, lacking both grace and the image of God.

In *The Trinity and the Kingdom* Moltmann speaks of two Trinities: economic and immanent. He says that "the 'economic Trinity' is the object of kerygmatic and practical theology; the 'immanent Trinity' the content of doxological theology."[17] The "economic" Trinity comes first because the praise of the "immanent" Trinity is dependent upon the gratitude of persons for the salvation in history which was accomplished by the "economic" Trinity. All the statements so far are about the economic Trinity. Moltmann's immanent Trinity is classical in that he uses the traditional names for the three persons, Father, Son, and Spirit. The distinctions are traditional also. The Father is the one who is "without origin"[18] and "he is the Father of the Son and the One who brings forth the Spirit."[19] Moltmann states clearly that the term Father is only theological and arises out of the relationship to the Son. The Son is the "'only begotten,' eternal Son of the Father,"[20] who is given everything by the Father except the Fatherhood. "The Spirit is 'breathed out' (spiration) not begotten (generation)."[21] Therefore the Spirit is not another Son. Also the Spirit proceeds only from the Father, else the Son would also be a Father. Here Moltmann is intentionally following the Orthodox way and denying the addition of "and the Son" *(filioque)* to the Nicene Creed by the West which supports the double procession of the Spirit from both the Father and the Son. The "and the Son" was added in the West to the paragraph on the Holy Spirit in the Nicene Creed so that it reads "We believe in the Holy Spirit, the Lord, the giver of life, who proceeds from the Father **and the Son**." This addition

[17] Ibid. 152.
[18] Ibid. 165.
[19] Ibid.
[20] Ibid. 166.
[21] Ibid. 169.

led the Western theologians to develop a doctrine of the Trinity that insisted on speaking of the Father and the Son together as the source for the Holy Spirit, thus called the double procession of the Spirit. This is a position the Eastern Orthodox have consistently denied. Moltmann does this because the *filioque* seems to add confusion to the careful distinctions he has made among the three persons of the Trinity.

Although Moltmann insists that the economic Trinity is the immanent Trinity and vice versa it appears that, as with Robert Jenson, such unity of these two Trinities is only an eschatological possibility. "The economic Trinity completes itself and perfects itself to immanent Trinity when the history and experience of salvation are completed and perfected. When everything is 'in God' and 'God is all in all,' then the economic Trinity is raised into and transcended in the immanent Trinity. What remains is the eternal praise of the Triune God in his glory."[22] Thus the coming together of the two Trinities only occurs in what Moltmann terms the kingdom of glory.

Moltmann's understanding of the kingdom of God is also Trinitarian. The kingdom of the Father includes the creation of the world and a presumed openness to the future as well as the preservation of existence which points to the kingdom of glory. The kingdom of the Son "consists of the liberating lordship of the crucified one, and fellowship with the first born of many brothers and sisters."[23] The kingdom of the Spirit "is experienced in the gift conferred on the people liberated by the Son . . . [and] is the anticipation of the eschatological indwelling of God's glory."[24] It is in the kingdom of glory that the creation will be perfected, and it is here that the goal for creation, the glorification of the Triune God, will be achieved so that the history of salvation finally culminates in "the eternally living Triune God who draws us into and includes us in his eternal triune life with all the fullness of its relationships"[25] and so brings about the experience of the salvation of the world.

In Moltmann's more recent works, *The Spirit of Life: A Universal Affirmation* and *The Coming of God: Christian Eschatology,* he speaks more about sanctification, the presence of God in the world, and our responsibility for creation. However, his emphasis on the future as the locus for the kingdom remains.

In *The Spirit of Life* Moltmann offers four Trinities: the monarchical, the historical, the eucharistic, and the doxological. The monarchical pattern for the Trinity is located in Western Christian thought. Moltmann claims that this Trinity is economic only since "there is in actual fact no

---

22 Ibid. 208.
23 Ibid. 210.
24 Ibid. 212.
25 Ibid. 157.

'immanent Trinity' at all which could exist independent in itself."[26] He names this Trinity the primordial Trinity since it is "open and prepared for revelation and salvation."[27] This is the Trinity that is responsible for sending the Son and Spirit into the world and for experiencing the creation as it acts on God.

The historical Trinity is the Trinity in a time sequence based on the work of Joachim of Fiore. The periods of salvation corresponding to the three persons of the Trinity are the period of Mosaic Law, the period "according to the Gospel of Christ" and the period in which "God will be directly known."[28]

The eucharistic Trinity follows the actions of the monarchical Trinity and the praise and thanksgiving received by the Trinity is in response to the salvation that God has accomplished in Christ. God as eucharistic Trinity receives rather than sends. Moltmann bases the relationship between these two Trinities on the Orthodox summary of salvation, i.e., "God became human so that human beings should be deified."[29] God comes to us in the primordial Trinity bringing salvation so that we can return to God in the eucharistic Trinity.

The last Trinity is the doxological Trinity which focuses on the equality of the members of the Trinity since all are worshiped and glorified together. Moltmann says that "'worship and glorification' go beyond the salvation that has been experienced and the thanksgiving that has been expressed."[30] Salvation is the product of the primordial and historical Trinities and thanksgiving is the expression of the eucharistic Trinity. Since this doxological Trinity is beyond the salvation accomplished by the "economic" Trinity, this Trinity is the "immanent" Trinity, that is, God related internally as Trinity by means of *perichoresis*.

In developing these four Trinities Moltmann makes explicit the relationship of God as Trinity to the world. This relationship is about salvation manifested in the primordial and the historical Trinities. This relationship also includes the response of humanity to God in the eucharistic Trinity and it tells us about God in God's own internal relationships within the doxological Trinity.

In this text Moltmann develops further the relationships in the Trinity particularly between Christ and the Spirit. He approaches this relationship from two perspectives. First is "The Christ of the Spirit." The Spirit is present

---

[26] Jürgen Moltmann, *The Spirit of Life: A Universal Affirmation,* tr. Margaret Kohl (Minneapolis: Fortress, 1992) 291, 292.

[27] Ibid. 292.

[28] Ibid. 297.

[29] Ibid. 299.

[30] Ibid. 301.

in the life of Israel in general and particularly in the ministry of John the Baptist before Jesus appears. It is through an experience of the Spirit that Jesus understood his own calling. It is by means of the indwelling of the Spirit that Jesus understands himself to be the "kingdom of God in person."[31] Moltmann adds quickly that this does not make him a "superman." This Spirit experiences Jesus' suffering, remaining with him through his death but without dying. This Spirit is not overwhelmed by these experiences "for he is Jesus' strength in suffering, and is even the 'indestructible life in whose power Jesus can give himself vicariously for many.'"[32] It is the presence of the Spirit that makes what appears to be an end into a new beginning. "The Spirit by participating in the death and resurrection of Christ becomes 'the Spirit of Christ (Rom 8.9), so that Christ becomes the determining subject of the Spirit . . . .'"[33] It is this Spirit that becomes the vitalizing energy that brings life to the whole creation and makes the world holy; this sanctification is possible because the Spirit brings about the new creation. The world and human beings are made holy by an act of God that establishes a relationship of love, so that whatever God loves is described as holy. This does not mean that the person or creature is holy in itself. It is possible to grow in holiness, but this holiness comes from the goodness of the person in response to the love of God who has already made the person holy in the relationship. Moltmann is clear that the goal of sanctification is to restore the image of God in which all human beings were created.

Moltmann extends the concept of sanctification beyond the individual to include relationships with other people and the world as an ecosystem. He claims that "today sanctification means integrating ourselves once more in the web of life from which modern society has isolated men and women and is separating them more and more."[34] This emphasis on relationship takes on a political dimension as it is broadened to include creation. As he says, "today sanctification means defending God's creation against human aggression, exploitation and destruction."

It is in his latest work, *The Coming of God,* that Moltmann again shows that eschatology is the foundation of his theology. He can and does speak of sanctification, and the participation of life in the divine life. He insists that eternal life is "not just life in 'the world beyond,' 'life after death;' it is an awakening, a rebirth, already here and now, and the endowment of earthly life with new vital energies."[35] But he also says that "eternal life al-

[31] Ibid. 61.

[32] Ibid. 64.

[33] Ibid. 68.

[34] Ibid. 172.

[35] Jürgen Moltmann, *The Coming of God: Christian Eschatology,* tr. Margaret Kohl (Minneapolis: Fortress, 1996) 337.

ready begins here and now in the midst of the life that is transitory, and makes of earthly life a prelude to itself,"[36] so that he is careful to speak of "preludes" and "foretastes" and "anticipation." When he speaks of the eschatological moment it is clear that this must be thought of as "beyond the end and consummation of history, as the consummation of creation-in-the-beginning and therefore as the exit from time into eternity."[37] It is important to note his more recent emphasis on what happens here and now and what the human responsibility for the creation is, yet his preoccupation with eschatology as that which happens beyond time rather than as the end time that becomes present in this time places the focus always in the future. This can be used to discount the importance of what is happening now, which he seems to want to avoid, but he is not convincing. In the paradox of the relationship between the kingdom of God as "already" and "not yet" the emphasis for Moltmann seems still to be on the "not yet."

Conclusion

Jürgen Moltmann has provided much that coincides with Orthodox theology, especially his understanding that the Trinity includes christology and soteriology as foundational. Ideas congruent with Orthodoxy include the paradigm of transfiguration as applied to the salvation of the world, the enlarged scope of salvation that includes the universe and not only human beings, the understanding that salvation begins with creation and not the fall, the realization that God limits God's power in order to make human freedom a reality, and the relationship between the persons of the Trinity as best described by *perichoresis*.

He adds to these ancient ideas the reciprocal relationship between God and the world so that the "economic Trinity," at least, is recipient of what occurs here on earth. He also adds the notion that time, and therefore change, are at the heart of the universe, and since the "economic Trinity" is the history of salvation, presumably time and change are included in God as well. All of the above will inform our own formulation of the doctrine of the Trinity.

Moltmann also contributes two major problems to the discussion. He describes a theology that, like Orthodoxy, refuses to address the "how is that possible?" question. He does not develop an operative metaphysics that can explain how this history of salvation actually occurs. The second problem stems from Moltmann's ever-present accent on eschatology. Salvation finally is something that happens in God in the kingdom of glory

[36] Ibid. 292.
[37] Ibid. 294.

when the economic and immanent Trinities are brought together, or when the four Trinities function together to bring about the kingdom of glory. The Son subjects himself to the Father and God becomes all in all. A function of this problem is that the universe that God so loves as to create and save it does not experience any of this saving activity until the end. Thus the kingdom of God in the world is never more than a hope. For all of Moltmann's language of time and change, such change as happens on earth is not fostered by or in response to a relationship to God until the eschaton. Moltmann enhances the concept of salvation by including the world; nevertheless, delaying the world's experience of salvation until the end causes the world to become devalued, for finally salvation will occur only in God. In our current context of ecological disasters, insisting that the world must wait until the eschaton to experience salvation may mean that we bring the eschaton on before God is ready! In his more recent works it is clear that he is aware of these issues, yet the emphasis on what happens beyond time is so heavy that this concern remains.

The concern for the salvation of the world as a currently occurring reality will be brought to our attention by feminist theology in the next chapter. The issue of a metaphysical undergirding will be addressed by process theology in the last two chapters.

Chapter Six

Feminism and the Doctrine of the Trinity

A Christian feminist critique of the classical Western doctrine of the Trinity will add to what Jürgen Moltmann has offered by being critical of areas that he ignored. It will be important to consider sin (especially original sin) and salvation from a feminist perspective, since these interpretations are quite different from those of Augustine, Barth, or Moltmann. In order for feminism to be a resource for constructing a doctrine of the Trinity that is integrative, its insights must be applied to the doctrines of God, Christ, and salvation, as well as the particular issue of language for God.

Feminist theology is a response to the patriarchal perspective of traditional theology. Patriarchy literally means "father-rule." This system of social organization locates power in the dominant man or men so that all others—women, children, slaves, non-dominant men—are clearly subordinate. The dominant men also have the power to determine the roles that everyone else will have in the system and the value assigned to these roles. In a culture that shows value by paying wages or salaries those jobs that have been determined to be women's work are consistently paid a lower wage, and women still earn 25 to 30 percent less than men in the same kinds of jobs.

This system claims that the man is the norm for the whole society so that any girl child born is from the beginning abnormal. As she grows she will learn that the language of this social structure reflects these power relationships. Thus until recently all references to someone in general were always "he." Now in some institutions there are guidelines for writing in inclusive language in an attempt to overcome the male bias of the language. Language referring to God is usually considered to be a special case in a way that makes the male as norm more difficult to challenge. The strength of this pattern is such that when the New Revised Standard Version of the Bible was published in 1991 all the pronouns referring to God remained male.

Considering women as abnormal or as defective men has a long tradition in philosophy and theology. It begins with Aristotle in the fourth century B.C.E. who claimed that every child should be male since the child is deposited whole by the male into the female who contributes nothing to the child except a warm, safe place to grow. This child should copy the father and be male but sometimes, possibly due to a south wind, the child will be a female, a defective male. This perspective influenced the early Christian theologians who wrote and interpreted biblical texts. The influence of this philosophy is apparent in the twelfth century when Thomas Aquinas again appealed to Aristotle in developing his own theology. The Roman Catholic Church still relies on the theology of Aquinas today, as it did in the response to the Protestant Reformation. Aquinas says that "only as regards nature in the individual is the female something defective and misbegotten."[1] Building on this assessment he determines that a woman's soul is deficient, her intellect is weak, and she will be easily manipulated. Hence she requires someone to take care of her, since she is not capable of caring for herself. These assumptions also lie behind English civil law that has tended to lump women, children, and imbeciles together in one category. These assumptions about women have led to denying women access to education, work, political participation, and leadership roles in the Church. Feminist critique of these assumptions challenges the whole patriarchal worldview, which is built on biases based on sex, race, heterosexuality, and economic class. The goal of feminists is to create a world based on relationships of interdependence and mutuality for all people.

Christian feminists have challenged the way the Bible has been translated and interpreted. They have done their own historical research to reveal a different picture of what the world looked like in the era of the early Church and they have constructed feminist Christian theologies. It is only in the past thirty years that women have been educated in the languages of the Scriptures (Hebrew, Greek, and Aramaic). With these tools women can now read the texts in the original languages and offer different translations and interpretations than those available to the tradition. For example, Bernadette J. Brooten has determined that the name of one of the persons greeted in Rom 16:7 is not Junias, but Junia.[2] This means that the transla-

---

[1] Elizabeth Johnson, *She Who Is* (New York: Crossroad, 1993) 24.

[2] "Junia . . . Outstanding Among the Apostles (Romans 16:7)," in Leonard Swidler and Arlene Swidler, eds., *Women Priests: A Catholic Commentary on the Vatican Declaration* (New York: Paulist, 1977).

tion of this passage has changed. In the RSV translation of the Bible this passage reads "Greet Andronicus and Junias, my kinsmen and my fellow prisoners; they are men of note among the apostles, and they were in Christ before me." The NRSV translation of the passage says "Greet Andronicus and Junia, my relatives who were in prison with me; they are prominent among the apostles, and they were in Christ before I was." The RSV account indicates that all of the participants are men. Brooten discovered that this change was made during the Middle Ages since early manuscripts and translations read Junia or Julia but clearly refer to this person as a woman. Brooten researched the history of the name Junias to see if it appeared with any regularity as a man's name and found no other instances of its use, while Junia was a common name for a woman. Her evidence was strong enough to convince the translators of the NRSV that the name should be changed. In the newer translation Junia is a woman and is named with Andronicus as "prominent among the apostles." Bringing a feminist perspective to this text meant not assuming that only men could be apostles, so the name must be a man's name, but instead being open to the possibility that women could also be apostles. Similar work has been done on Genesis 2–3 by Old Testament scholars like Phyllis Trible[3] and Beverly Stratton.[4] This passage is particularly important because it is on the basis of these chapters that women have been blamed for bringing evil into the world and the claim that women should be subordinate is also in this text.

Elisabeth Schüssler Fiorenza[5] and Karen Jo Torjesen[6] have both explored the era of the New Testament texts. Fiorenza argues for a period of time in the early Church when men *and* women were leaders. She follows Paul in Galatians where he says "there is no longer Jew or Greek, there is no longer slave or free, there is no longer male and female for all of you are one in Christ Jesus" (Gal 3:28). She claims that the patriarchy of the Church came about by its capitulation to the Roman Empire, which had a clearly patriarchal structure at that time. Torjesen has uncovered evidence that women were priests during this early era which is the basis of her book *When Women Were Priests*. These feminist historians have put women back into the Christian story and have shown that the hierarchical

[3] Phyllis Trible, *God and the Rhetoric of Sexuality* (Philadelphia: Fortress, 1978).

[4] Beverly J. Stratton, *Out of Eden: Reading, Rhetoric, and Ideology in Genesis 2–3*. JSOT.S 28 (Sheffield: Sheffield Academic Press, 1995).

[5] Elisabeth Schüssler Fiorenza, *In Memory of Her: A Feminist Theological Reconstruction of Christian Origins* (New York: Crossroad, 1983).

[6] Karen Jo Torjesen, *When Women Were Priests: Women's Leadership in the Early Church and the Scandal of their Subordination in the Rise of Christianity* (San Francisco: HarperSan Francisco, 1993).

structure with which most of us are familiar was not the original structure of the Church. The result of work by feminist biblical scholars and feminist historians is that feminist theologians have been able to construct feminist theology. The goal of feminist theology is not to "add women and stir" into a patriarchal, biased system, but to write theology in a way that transforms the theological system that in turn will transform the social, cultural system.

Feminist theology is consciously based on women's experience of God and the world since God is revealed in and through the world to women as well as to men. Women experience the world as the appropriate place to live, work, raise families, educate, transmit values, and in so doing change the world. Feminist orientation is toward the world and toward the future that holds promises that require an investment of concern, time, and energy to be brought to realization. Therefore a feminist understanding of salvation is this-worldly. It can be described as transformation or healing. This healing is not only for women and men but for the earth as well. Salvation is about changing the world—its policies, ideas, relationships of power, and economics—so that the future is one of promise and hope, but it is brought about by people who join together in community in order to facilitate healthy relationships between persons, communities, and nations. The reign of God that is promised is already active in the world and not only a future, awaited event. The interest of feminists in salvation focuses on this world now and in the imminent future rather than accepting suffering in the present in the hope for a better experience someplace else or in some remote time in the future when healing will take place.

Women experience the world as interrelated or interconnected. What women do affects the lives of our family, friends, community, world, and God, and it is in this connectedness that women and men experience community and strength. This connectedness makes it impossible to entertain a notion of salvation that includes anything less than the whole cosmos. Salvation is an inclusive concept that encompasses life and health for all. It is not possible to speak of one or a few persons being healed while condemning the rest to suffering or brokenness, nor can one speak of healing humanity apart from healing the Earth. Eco-feminism has developed because of the recognition of the fact that the way women have been, and are, treated is parallel to the way the earth has been devalued, used, and discarded. In order for salvation to occur the dualism that keeps God separate from the world must be overcome.

Again, based on the experience of women the definition of sin usually employed by male theologians is not descriptive of the primary issue for women. Pride (or power over) is truly a description of the sin of those who have power over others and over the world. Those who have this power are tempted to "pride," a desire for control that destroys relationships. But in this patriarchal culture women generally do not have power over others, so that pride is not their primary temptation. They have been so denigrated in the process of being acculturated as female that they have little if any pride in being women or in the gifts and talents they have to contribute to the world.

Sin for women consists in accepting the patriarchal culture's definition of "woman" and the presumed limitations of intelligence and ability that are central to that definition. Thus for women overcoming sin and enjoying salvation require redefinition of what it means to be woman in a way that celebrates women's intelligence, talents, and abilities. Women as well as men must recognize that these talents and abilities are necessary for the salvation of the world that includes men and women. Salvation requires the overcoming of the male/female dualism that is so ingrained in our culture. Interdependence means that we are going to be healed or broken together.

Salvation is thus a process of liberation from bondage to a system that abuses and traps women in a stereotype that serves the patriarchal structure and requires women to be obedient to this system. Theology can either support the patriarchal system or support the liberation of women and men. There is no neutral theology capable of taking a nonpolitical position. Theology is necessarily political. For women it is clear that the process of liberation is of God and that the patriarchal commands to obedience are man-made; they serve not to bring healing and wholeness to people or the world but to keep those privileged by the system in power. Therefore salvation is a process of transforming the world in a way that recognizes our interdependence, liberates those who are trapped by sexism, heterosexism, racism, and classism, and heals those who are broken.

This process of liberation needs to begin by examining the powerful words that are used to describe who God is and how God acts in the world. That God has been imaged in almost exclusively male terms throughout the history of Judaism and Christianity is a major issue for women. College students still persist in assuming that God is an old white man with a long white beard who sits on a golden throne. Some will even admit to a close parallel between this image of God and Santa Claus. The Christian image of God as Father has been identified with the feudal Lord or imperial Caesar who rules by fiat and for whom power as control is the most important attribute. This has led the Church, on occasion, to teach that men are created in the image of God but women are not and that women therefore must become "men" in order to be saved. Normally men act in the place of God in the family, so that all persons in that family are to be obedient to the father as representative of God. Similarly all are to be obedient to their king or other male rulers as standing in the place of God. This assumed power by men and assumed subservience of women have led to the abuse of women and children, who are considered property, and are linked together because they have often been legally and politically powerless.

The image of God as male leads to the image of the male as God (Mary Daly).[7] This connection assumes that any language that names God will be male language. This image is so powerful that while the New Revised Standard Version of the Bible in 1991 recognized the male bias in the Greek language and changed "brothers" to "sisters and brothers," the language about God was not changed. However, the issue of what language to use to name God is being contested in most denominations at this time.

Robert Jenson represents one end of the spectrum: God's proper name is Father and thus the language that refers to the Trinity can only be Father, Son, and Holy Spirit. There are no acceptable alternatives. At the other end of this spectrum is a constant experimenting with vocabulary without any attempt at theological integration of doctrines of which this language is the result. Jürgen Moltmann represents a middle position and is the only male theologian here considered who seriously considers options to the traditional language and images. Many theologians wrote before this issue was being raised and so cannot be faulted. However, those who have written since 1985 certainly need to demonstrate that they are aware of the issue. Jenson shows both his awareness and his unwillingness to change. Not only is his language about God male only, his entire text is written in exclusively male language.

As is frequently the case most Christian churches are somewhere in the middle. Attempts at inclusive God-language are made during the general liturgy or worship service. The most commonly used alternative language is Creator, Redeemer, and Sustainer. Others say Father/Mother, Son/Daughter, Spirit/Sustainer. Women who have offered options include Letty Russell, who conceives the Trinity as "Creator, Liberator, and Advocate who calls human beings into partnership with divine care for the world,"[8] and Hildegard of Bingen, a twelfth-century mystic who spoke of the Trinity as "a brightness, a flashing forth and a fire."[9] Another method is to employ verbs and so to speak of God who creates, redeems, and sanctifies.

While all these options are used during worship, the compromise with those in Jenson's position occurs when the sacrament of baptism is celebrated. During this event the usual practice is to do as the gospel of Matthew directs and baptize in the name of the Father, the Son, and the Holy Spirit. Some denominations have mandated this practice, meaning

[7] Mary Daly, *Beyond God the Father: Toward a Philosophy of Women's Liberation* (Boston: Beacon Press, 1973; London: The Women's Press, 1986) 138.

[8] Johnson, *She Who Is* 210.

[9] Ibid. 211.

that no alternative language is permitted. A compromise solution is to use alternative language such as Creator, Christ, and Holy Spirit, and then add "which the tradition names as Father, Son, and Holy Spirit." This practice both acknowledges the tradition of the Church and shows awareness that this tradition is perceived to have limitations in the present.

Women will continue this struggle over language because exclusively male language has been at the root of the exclusion of women from leadership positions in the Church. It has been supportive of the cultural practice of treating women as property, along with children, and viewing them as incapable of making intelligent, responsible decisions. The exclusively male imagery of God has made it possible for male theologians to argue for the subservience of women to men, causing women who grow up in the Church to assume they are inferior to men in intelligence and abilities. The Church, when it insists on maintaining male-only imagery and language for God, continues to contribute to the low self-esteem already inflicted upon women by the culture. Such language sides with the powerful against the powerless. In the Christian tradition there has always been an acknowledgment that God is actually beyond human comprehension so that any language about God is inadequate. Exclusively male language for God is therefore idolatrous in that it insists that this is accurate language rather than admitting that this language is also by way of analogy and metaphor. Since the power of this language is now evident, any doctrine of the Trinity developed for this time and in this present context of awareness of the power of language will need to find language that is inclusive or that at least is not exclusive of either men or women.

A feminist critique of the doctrine of God that goes with exclusively male language calls into question the presumption that power as control is God's most important attribute and that this is the way God relates to the world. Feminists suggest including feminine images of God, e.g., Mother, with its attendant properties of nurturing, caring, loving, encouraging, and life-giving, to offset and redefine the all-powerful, controlling Father-God. Since salvation for feminists is a joint project between God and humanity, God is not portrayed as all-powerful. Since it occurs in the world and not someplace else and since it is now and not at some other time, salvation is a process of transforming the world.

The Christian tradition has often supported male privilege in the Church based on the fact that Jesus was male and that he presumably chose only male disciples. Some feminists have given up on Christianity, considering it so patriarchal as to be beyond change, and have become post-Christian precisely over this issue. They cannot accept that a male can be the savior for women, and they certainly cannot take part in a Church in which they are relegated on theological grounds to a subordinate role.

Feminists who remain Christian have developed a hermeneutics of suspicion to be applied especially when reading biblical texts. This approach
acknowledges the power the patriarchal culture had in Judaism and in the
Roman Empire during the lifetime of Jesus and in the period during which
the New Testament was written and compiled. This way of interpreting
Scripture tries to separate the gospel, the good news in Christ, from its patriarchal context so that in telling the story of Jesus it is not necessary to
support the patriarchal culture. They recognize that in that culture only a
male could have gone about preaching as Jesus did and only males could
have been chosen to represent the twelve tribes of Israel; therefore it is not
surprising that the gospel accounts name only men as disciples.

Christian feminists take special note of the Scriptural texts in which
Jesus interacts with women because his actions are not typical of Jewish
males of that era. Jesus does not avoid women, even Gentile women. Jesus
speaks to women, listens to women (Luke 7:36-50), teaches women (Luke
10:38-42), learns from women (Mark 7:24-30), heals women (Mark 5:25-
34; Luke 13:10-17) and their daughters (Mark 5:21-43), has compassion
on women (Luke 7:11-17; John 7:53–8:11), and women witness to Jesus
as the Christ (John 4:1-42). In every gospel text it is the women who go to
the tomb on Easter morning and find it empty. Feminists interpret the behavior of Jesus toward women as signaling a new way for men and women
to relate to each other, a new way that is underscored by Paul in his letter
to the Galatians.

This new relationship overcomes the old patterns of clean/unclean,
Jew/Gentile, slave/free, male/female because "you are all one in Christ
Jesus" (Gal 3:28). Therefore the function of Jesus as the Christ is to embody God's relationship to the world so that we can see that God is about
liberating oppressed persons from the oppressors whether that oppression
is based on economics or race or sexuality or gender. Jesus brings all
people into the sphere of participation that continues the salvation of the
world. The story of the life of Jesus is significant because it tells us how
God relates to the world and because it tells us how we can relate to the
world in a way that is healing and not destructive. We can do what Christ
did in Jesus because we are like Jesus and have the same possibility of relating to the world as he did. The story of Jesus is also a warning that the
world is not hospitable to being turned upside down and being restructured
in an egalitarian way. Thus Jesus was put to death by a fearful Roman gov-
ernment. That God responded to this tragedy by raising Jesus to new life
is indicative of God's relationship to the world. God cannot prevent
tragedies, but God can respond in ways that share the pain and bring about
healing. What Jesus did is not done once for all but is the paradigm of
what all followers of Christ need to be about in order to bring healing and

wholeness to a divided world. Followers can have the same confidence in the presence of God that Jesus had in contributing to the transformation of the world, but also need to be wise to the ways of the world and the price that it may demand.

Feminists are aware of the power of language and are aware of the impact that images we apply to God have on our lives. Therefore one of the primary concerns in relation to the doctrine of the Trinity is to develop language for God that avoids both power images and maleness. Recently Sallie McFague has made a major contribution to renaming the Trinity in her book *Models of God*. The metaphors for God offered by McFague are models that come from our experience and help us talk about God. They are not intended to exhaust or limit the reality that is God since that reality is beyond articulation.

McFague's primary metaphor is the world as God's body; it is where God is actualized. This world is the beloved of God. This view requires that we reassess the value placed on the world because as God's body it now has infinite value for us and for God. It also means that God needs the world if God is to be actualized and to be in relationship with anything outside of God. Also implied is the realization that "God needs us to help save the world."[10] The persons of the Trinity are ordered according to the three words for love in the Greek language: *agapē, erōs*, and *philia*.

The first person is associated with *agapē* and reflects love for the world that is freely given and expects nothing in return. McFague's term for this person is Mother because this person is the giver of life. "Parental love is the most powerful and intimate experience we have of giving love whose return is not calculated."[11] Her reason for using Mother rather than Father for this first person is because "what the father-God gives is redemption from sins; what the mother-God gives is life itself."[12] This lifegiving is not dispassionate as *agapē* has been previously considered; rather this mother's love shows concern and caring for all creatures and for the whole Earth; concern that they all live and will be reunited to the source of their life.

McFague moves away from the problem/solution motif so common in Western Christian theology. She prefers mother-God to father-God because father-God assumes a need to bring in an expert and rescue people. Mother-God as creator is concerned to achieve "the just ordering of the cosmic household in a fashion beneficial to all."[13] This mother-God is not primarily judge of those who disobey; instead she desires with our cooperation to create "a just ecological economy for the well-being of all her

[10] Sallie McFague, *Models of God* (Philadelphia: Fortress, 1987) 103.

[11] Ibid. 103.

[12] Ibid. 101.

[13] Ibid. 117.

creatures."[14] This relationship of God to the world means that we need to change our attitude toward the world. It is no longer ours to dominate, use, and throw away. The world is our joint creation with God and our role becomes one of "preservers, those who pass life along and who care for all forms of life so they may prosper."[15]

The second person is imaged as *erōs* or lover. McFague recognizes that while the Scripture attests to God as love, the Church has been unwilling to speak of God as lover because this implies that God needs the world and has passion toward the world. Yet it is love with passion or the desire to be with the beloved that gives value to the beloved. This is the heart of the issue and precisely why the image of God as lover is appropriate. Just as God lives in God's body, so God lives in each of us because we have been created in the image of God. For McFague this gives us a positive image of ourselves that is opposed to the depraved sinner image in some popular Protestant theology. In light of this change salvation is no longer understood as a rescue mission to pluck us out of this terrible place, something that happens to only a chosen few for reasons we cannot know. Rather "the model of God as lover implies that salvation is the reunification of the beloved world with its lover God."[16] We are necessary to this process, for it is in and through us that the salvation of the world is possible. Note that salvation is only spoken of in a cosmic dimension. It is not possible with this model to isolate people or nations, to save some and condemn others. We are all in this together and our choices are in terms of participating in the salvation of the world or remaining isolated from others and thwarting salvation.

Sin is no longer defined as being disobedient to God or injuring God. Sin is defined in terms of what does or does not happen in relationships in the world. Therefore "sin is the turning-away not from a transcendent power but from interdependence with all other beings, including the matrix of being from whom all life comes. It is not pride or unbelief but the refusal of relationship."[17] Sin can also be defined in terms of refusing to participate with God. This refusal, McFague writes, is "in our model the definition of sin, the refusal to be the special part of creation, of God's body, that we are called to be—namely, those who among the beloved can respond to God as lover by working to reunite and heal the fragmented world."[18]

God as lover does not coerce us into participating but lures us into cooperation by gracious love and tenderness. This lover recognizes and hon-

---

[14] Ibid. 117.
[15] Ibid. 122.
[16] Ibid. 135.
[17] Ibid. 139.
[18] Ibid. 136.

ors our freedom to ignore the offer of love and relationship. This second person is identified with Jesus only in that Jesus is a paradigmatic figure for us. Everyone has the potential to be a sign of God the lover by being open and responsive to God. "Jesus' response as beloved to God as lover was so open and thorough that his life and death were revelatory of God's great love for the world."[19] McFague insists that Jesus is not "ontologically different from other paradigmatic figures . . . who manifest in word and deed the love of God for the world."[20] The function of Jesus is not to do something for us but to show us what we need to be doing for ourselves and for the world.

The third person of this Trinity is God as friend, from the Greek word *philia*. "Friendship at its most elemental is the bonding of two people by free choice in a reciprocal relationship."[21] The basis of friendship is freedom. There is no sense of duty or of using the other person for one's own ends. A friend is someone you like who likes you back. It is frequently a bond of a shared world view that brings and keeps people together. This shared vision is what is most important in the divine-human friendship because it "frees friendship from the self-absorbed individualism of its classical roots."[22] While this definition is more inclusive it does not lose sight of the fact that "one still chooses freely and out of a sense of joy to join with God the friend in a mutual project of great interest to both: the well being of the world."[23] This is the third way in which God relates to the world and it also describes how we relate to the world. The point is to describe a nonhierarchical relationship. If this mutual relationship is possible between God and the world, surely it is possible between humans and the world. This is a description of salvation as a process of befriending the world. We arc part of this process. The goal is to overcome all dualisms: divine/human, male/female, and human/world.

Conclusion

Sallie McFague has used the doctrine of the Trinity to outline a feminist way to describe the relationship of God and the world. Her theology is clearly feminist in that it is based on women's experience of God and women's experience of the world. She has paid attention to redefining the classical understanding of salvation in a way that is consistent with the feminist understanding described earlier. This required redefining sin, and

[19] Ibid.
[20] Ibid.
[21] Ibid. 160.
[22] Ibid. 163.
[23] Ibid.

also who Jesus was and what he was about. She expanded our thought about God by using new terms—Mother, Lover, Friend—to describe God's relationship to the world. All of this carefully-thought-out discussion supports a feminist theological world view.

Each of her expressions for God is related to the salvation of the world. Her discussion of God as lover includes an understanding of what the role of Jesus is in this theology. She is, however, not attempting to develop a doctrine of God since she claims to be proposing models for thinking of God rather than offering a description of God or hypotheses about God's nature. All of her models are in terms of God "as" Mother, Lover, Friend. There is therefore no doctrine of God as such operating in this system. There is no statement that "God is . . . ." The object is to redefine how God relates to the world and to be clear that this relationship is one that brings about the possibility of salvation. This McFague has accomplished. The choice to base her system on the three Greek words for love seems arbitrary, but perhaps no more arbitrary than the doctrine of the Trinity in Western Christian theology in general.

A second feminist theologian who has developed a Trinity based on a feminist theology is Elizabeth Johnson. She claims that ". . . in the living tradition I believe that we need a strong dose of female imagery to break the unconscious sway that male trinitarian imagery holds over the imaginations of even the most sophisticated thinkers."[24] Johnson builds on her fundamental idea of God as wisdom, *sophia*. Therefore the three persons of the Trinity are God as Spirit-Sophia, God as Jesus Christ, Sophia's child, and God as Holy Wisdom.

God as Spirit-Sophia is the "mobile, pure, people-loving Spirit who pervades every wretched corner, wailing at the waste, releasing power that enables fresh starts."[25] She permeates the earth and the heavens, including each person, providing the energy for life.

In the second person She is incarnate in Jesus, who was not sent by Holy Wisdom to die but to demonstrate a new way to live, a way of compassion in solidarity with the poor and outcasts. "The crucified Jesus embodies the exact opposite of the patriarchal ideal of the powerful man, and shows the steep price to be paid in the struggle for liberation. The cross thus stands as a poignant symbol for the 'kenosis of patriarchy,' the self-emptying of male dominating power in favor of the new humanity of compassionate service and mutual empowerment. On this reading Jesus' maleness is prophecy announcing the end of patriarchy, at least as divinely ordained."[26] Given this understanding it is not so much a problem that

[24] Johnson, *She Who Is* 212.
[25] Ibid. 213.
[26] Ibid. 161.

Jesus was male as it is a problem that more men do not understand what he was doing and follow him. Jesus-Sophia is the Christ because he has been anointed by the Spirit. For Johnson the concept of Christ includes Jesus, but also all who participate in the Spirit. There is an eschatological dimension as well. This same Spirit raises Jesus into glory. Exactly what this means is beyond comprehension, but it points toward a transformation of humanity. If both the inclusiveness of Christ and the eschatological dimension of Christ are taken into account, the maleness of Jesus is not a problem because it refers only to his "sex as an intrinsic part of his own particular identity as a finite human being in time and space."[27]

The third person is God as Holy Wisdom who "is the matrix of all that exists, mother and fashioner of all things, who herself dwells in light inaccessible."[28] She is hidden and a complete and holy mystery. She is incarnate in this historical process that desires the healing and liberation of the world. These three persons are the Trinity. The internal relations are described as "the livingness of unoriginate Mother, her beloved Child, and the Spirit of their mutual love; or the vitality of Wisdom's abyss, her personal word and her energy; or Sophia's eternal communion in personal mystery, hidden, uttered, and bestowed; or the relations of Spirit, Wisdom and Mother in encircling movement." This Trinity is designed to affirm that SHE WHO IS, Johnson's name for God, is not a solitary entity but is always in relationship and that relationship is mutual. There is no hierarchy or subordination in this relationship. These relationships are those of friendship. The role of the Trinity is to provide a paradigm of living that is mutual, connected, loving, and inclusive. "The point of all of these theological constructions is to give voice to fragmentary saving experiences as experiences of God, in the living tradition of the Christian story."[29]

This feminist theology contributes a new vision of the relationship of God and the world, one that includes God within the world without identifying God with the world. God is no longer all-powerful, rescuing people from an undesirable or evil world. Instead God is aligned with the world so that for us to relate to the world rightly is to do so in a way that brings about healing, the realization of interdependence and the cosmic dimension of salvation. It is this salvific relationship that makes it necessary to redefine the role of Jesus and the role that we play in this continuing saga. That McFague and Johnson are able seriously to suggest using the image of mother-God instead of father-God adds to our criteria the importance of the language by which we image God. They naturally use inclusive language

27 Ibid. 163.
28 Ibid. 214.
29 Ibid. 222.

for people as did this entire chapter on feminism. This is indicative of the attention that must be given to our language and images. Thus any reworking of a theological doctrine must mean recognizing the power of language, the context of theology, and the interrelatedness of who Jesus is as the Christ, what is salvation, and our understanding of God as Trinity. These important additions will be carried forward in the following chapters.

Chapter Seven

Process Theologians and the Trinity

Process theology offers a metaphysical understanding of the world that undergirds many feminist insights and some of Moltmann's ontology, while it shares the critique with both of these of some aspects of the Western Augustinian tradition. This chapter will introduce process thought and then survey what three process theologians (Norman Pittenger, Lewis Ford, and Joseph Bracken) have said about the Trinity.

Process theology is based on the philosophy of Alfred North Whitehead, a mathematician and philosopher who wrote his primary works during the 1920s. This is an integrated view of God and the world that Whitehead calls a cosmology. It can also be called a metaphysics since the worldview encompasses a description of the world that includes everything from subatomic particles to God and the universe. This cosmology was developed in response to traditional Western theology and Newtonian science, which by the 1920s was being challenged by Einstein and the ideas of relativity and quantum mechanics. Process thought draws upon insights from Scripture, theology, philosophy, the sciences, art, and history in an effort to construct a Christian theology.

Whitehead employs concepts from Plato and defines his own vocabulary. Actually Whitehead commented that all philosophy is really a footnote to Plato. The realm that Plato describes as the forms or ideals Whitehead labels real. These real ideas are abstract and are only encountered in the world when they become concrete or actual. For example, the color blue is real. It is an abstract, general idea. If someone says "the boy I am talking about is the one there in the blue shirt," that is probably enough of a description. The blue shirt may be in actuality navy blue, cerulean blue, baby blue, or slate blue. We encounter the general notion "blue" only in the blue shirt as it is actualized in each concrete, particular instance, although we would all insist that we know what is meant by "blue." "Blue" in this example is real, while the blue shirt is actual. In process thought these terms have specific meanings and are not interchangeable as they are sometimes used in general speech.

Whitehead views the world as a process of energy events that are constantly coming into being and perishing. Each of these energy events is called an "actual occasion." These occasions participate in their own creation by combining their past with a choice of future possibilities available in that instant. Once the occasion becomes concrete it perishes and becomes part of the past of the next forming actual occasion. The role of time is important, and time can only move from past to present to future. Whitehead's concern with time, and his view of the world as composed of energy events, represent a move to ground theology in contemporary physics rather than relying on the Newtonian physics that is assumed in a substance-based cosmology. Each actual occasion has a physical pole and a mental pole. This construction explains how it is possible for some events merely to repeat themselves (rock, table), while others are able to accept novel possibilities and make significant changes over time. In a rock the mental pole is so insignificant that there is no perceptible change, while in a dog, dolphin, or human the mental pole is so significant that these organisms are capable of learning and change. Thus as the mental pole activity increases the organisms become more complex.

For Whitehead God is necessary to this system as the source of vision and novelty for each energy event. God is related to the world by entertaining the long-range vision and by providing novelty in the world through the presentation of novel possibilities for the occasions that Whitehead calls initial aims. In this way God enters into the world and influences what happens in the world. God also feels the world through these occasions, and in the act of perishing each occasion enters into God to be preserved there everlastingly. Therefore the world is in God. Like all actual occasions, God has a mental pole and a physical pole. God in the world is the mental pole of God and is named the Primordial Nature of God. The physical pole is the world in God, which is named the Consequent Nature of God. The difference is in the sequential order of the poles. For actual occasions experience begins with the physical pole, which includes the past. Change is therefore very difficult because the power of the past is very strong. For God the mental pole, which provides novelty and change, comes first. It is possible for God to potentially envision a future and then to provide the best possibility to each actual occasion through its mental pole. This best possibility is not necessarily actualized in the world, because occasions have freedom. This freedom is exercised by each occasion as it chooses what from its past will be continued and as it chooses whether or not to accept the best possible future or something less. God is related to the world by luring the occasions into the best possible future by means of persuasion. Due to the freedom inherent in the system, God in process thought cannot act coercively on the world.

In process thought God and the world require each other. God is necessary for the world in order to provide possible futures and novelty. The world is necessary to God in order for anything, including God, to exist in actuality, or concretely. In God's relationship to the world God interacts with the world events and takes the perishing occasions into the Consequent Nature of God, which is concrete. This Nature also reconciles the events and saves all that is possible everlastingly.

Whitehead provided the categories for this cosmology, but he did not fully develop a Christian theology. Thus Christian theologians have employed process thought to inform and aid in understanding and constructing Christian theology. The following three process thinkers are also Christian theologians who have used process thought as a means for exploring the meaning of the doctrine of the Trinity.

Norman Pittenger wrote *The Divine Triunity* in response to a request. In this text he seeks to find a way to speak of the Triunity from a process perspective. The Trinity or "Triunity" is a received doctrine from the Christian tradition that is abstract and confusing in the Western tradition, and Pittenger wants to employ process thought to make this doctrine more contemporary. He is clear that the doctrine comes first and that process thought will be used in service of the doctrine. Pittenger is also writing in response to Cyril Richardson's claim that the doctrine of the Trinity, while acceptable for liturgy, is unhelpful theologically because it does not accurately reflect that God is only transcendent and immanent. In order to restore the third member of the Trinity Pittenger adds "concomitant" to transcendent and immanent, which adds the notion of God alongside of and with the creation.[1] He is also trying to bring together three types of religious teachings that have been emphasized at different historical times and at particular places. He identifies God as creator with the Deists, God as revealer with the humanists, and God as inspirer with the experiential tradition. His claim is that all three contribute to our understanding of God's relationship within God's self and to the world.

Pittenger sets the stage for discussing his specific triunitarian picture of God by describing the context as panentheistic. His world view is one in which "'everything has its existence in God but yet is not to be taken as

---

[1] W. Norman Pittenger, *The Divine Triunity* (Philadelphia: UCC Press, 1977) 102.

identical with God'. Or we might say that this is a position which sees God in everything. . . ."[2] He takes the time to describe this world view because "only in a panentheistic context can we satisfactorily find a way for the retaining of the inherited Trinitarian picture of God—or so I am convinced."[3]

Pittenger formulates his Triunity in terms of Parent (also Lover), Word, and Holy Spirit. God is Parent because God is "the everlastingly creative energy who works anywhere and everywhere, yet without denying the reality of creaturely freedom."[4] God as "self-expressive Word"[5] is the one who "acts with and beside his creation, by luring it and attracting it toward realizing its possibilities."[6] The Holy Spirit is God as the "Responsive Agency"[7] who is "active in and through his creation in its accepting or 'prehending' the lure or attraction which is offered to it, and thereby perfecting and heightening the intensity of its life and achieving fulfillment or satisfaction through a response which is richer and more adequate than the possibilities available through creaturely action alone. . . ."[8]

Pittenger does indeed use "process" terminology and requires a panentheistic world view; however, he shows his Western bias by expressing his preference for "triunity" instead of Trinity. This is better, he says, because "to talk of 'trinity' may very well suggest to some a tritheistic view of God . . . which would be the contradiction of the essential monotheism . . . which is fundamental to the entire Jewish-Christian development of religious insight, understanding and interpretation. But to say 'triunity' is to speak of oneness *and* threeness. . . ."[9] With this as a starting point Pittenger does not feel compelled to work particularly hard at showing how the three are one since for him the one is never clearly distinguished as three. His work is commendable as the first attempt at dealing with the Trinity in the context of a process cosmology. However, his assumptions are not only process ones, but are also clearly Western and Augustinian. Indeed, his own claim is to use process thought to clarify the received doctrine of the Triunity. Hence the Trinity does not serve, for Pittenger, the function that it did originally, for there is no attempt to integrate a process understanding of salvation, christology, and God into a Triunity. This understanding of the Triunity is developed separately from these other doctrines in the Augustinian manner. His major contribution is in terms

[2] Ibid. 93.
[3] Ibid. 95.
[4] Ibid. 116.
[5] Ibid.
[6] Ibid.
[7] Ibid.
[8] Ibid.
[9] Ibid. 11.

of offering the panentheistic worldview as the appropriate context for Trinitarian theology.

While Pittenger was the first process thinker to discuss the doctrine of the Trinity, he has been followed by others. Lewis Ford in the seventh chapter of his book *The Lure of God* also offers a triune understanding of God. Ford rejects the Western Trinitarian formula of one substance in three persons in favor of "a stricter reading more in accordance with the Greek fathers, 'one actuality having three distinct aspects.'"[10] This vocabulary places more emphasis on the three and relies on unity as sufficient to express one actuality. Ford is able to identify more closely with the Eastern (Greek) conceptuality because he operates with a process metaphysics. This enables him to say that "in contrast to Aristotle's dictum that one substance (i.e. actuality) cannot be in another, Whitehead's philosophy is designed to show how this may be so. One actuality, as concretum, can be objectively present in the concrescence of another."[11]

The advantage process theologians have over those who do not operate with a Whiteheadian metaphysics is that process theologians are able to say "three in one" and mean it concretely. Ford's Trinity consists of the "divine creative act nontemporally generating the primordial nature from which proceeds the consequent nature. . . ."[12] Ford identifies the "divine creative act" as the transcendent aspect and the "primordial nature" as the immanent aspect. If this Trinity were classically Western this would be sufficient, and Richardson's argument would have ended the discussion. However, in process philosophy transcendence and immanence are categories applied to the world as well as to God. Whitehead states, "it is as true to say that the World is immanent in God as that God is immanent in the World. It is as true to say that God transcends the World as that the World transcends God."[13] Therefore what is required is an aspect of God that "has the capacity to receive into itself the objective immanence of the world."[14] This is the consequent nature of God.

The primary problem with this particular construct is Ford's identification of the "primordial nature of God" with the Logos that is present in Jesus Christ. This Primordial Nature is "eternal, actually deficient and unconscious,"[15] so presence of the Logos in the world would not actualize the presence of God since it remains actually deficient. While Ford has con-

[10] Lewis Ford, *The Lure of God* (Philadelphia: Fortress, 1978) 101.
[11] Ibid. 102.
[12] Ibid.
[13] Alfred North Whitehead, *Process and Reality* (New York: The Free Press, 1978) 528.
[14] Ford, *The Lure of God* 109.
[15] Whitehead, *Process and Reality* 345. This is part of his description of the primordial nature of God.

tributed the important aspect of God's consequent nature as God who receives into God's self the feelings of the world, his construction of the Trinity is inadequate because it cannot clearly address the actuality in the world of the presence of God who is bringing about salvation in the world now.

The final process Trinitarian construction to be considered is offered by Joseph Bracken in his book *The Triune Symbol: Persons, Process and Community.* Bracken relies on process thought to define what he means by person as distinguished from individual. A person is always related to a community and is conscious of being internally related to all other persons in the community. This community ideally increases to encompass the world. An individual, on the contrary, is separate from any other individual and does not necessarily value relatedness, so that autonomy and self-sufficiency are most valued. This individual sees himself or herself defined as over against a society. Both "individual" and "society" are static concepts.

Bracken builds on the notions of person and community to be able to say that "Father, Son and Holy Spirit constitute a divine community."[16] He consistently argues against tritheism by means of the person-community relationship, "a union established which is simultaneously a matter of free choice for the members and yet distinctively interpersonal."[17]

Bracken follows process thought by making change normative even in God. This change is one-directional; "the three divine persons are constantly changing in their relationship to one another but always in the direction of a deeper and richer union."[18] His christology also reflects process thinking: "one major reason for the incarnation of the Son of God within the process perspective . . . was the need for a concrete model of human personhood, someone specifically to embody what the Father has in mind for all of us."[19]

This includes the possibility that each individual will respond positively to the best possibility for him or her in each instant given by the Father. Process theology names these possibilities initial aims. "The Father is the transcendent source of the initial aims communicated to each creature from moment to moment."[20] Each creature's response is free and open, so that God lures creatures into cooperation. God does not coerce creatures into unreflective obedience. This means, however, that "once again we are con-

---

[16] Joseph A. Bracken, *The Triune Symbol: Persons, Process, and Community* (New York: University Press of America, 1985) 87.

[17] Ibid. 17.

[18] Ibid. 27.

[19] Ibid. 89.

[20] Ibid. 87.

fronted with the sobering notion that human beings can use their personal freedom to thwart the divine plan for the salvation of the world. . . ."[21]

Bracken begins *The Triune Symbol* with the three and desires to explain how they are one. In this way he develops an excellent understanding of community. He takes issue with the usual definition of community as "a network of relationships between separate individuals who are first and foremost themselves and only in the second place associated with one another."[22] As Bracken continues he points out the worldview that is the assumption behind this understanding of community. It is that of Aristotle, and then in the Middle Ages of Thomas Aquinas. According to this view "only the individual entities ultimately exist."[23]

Given this worldview in which the individual is primary, God is also viewed as primarily one. What happens then is that one begins with the One (which is the traditional Western way) and then attempts to derive the Three from the One. Bracken acknowledges that this is what Aquinas tries, and he considers his attempt a failure in that Aquinas sacrifices the strictly personal character of the three divine persons as they relate each to the other.[24] In order to be able to begin with the three persons, as the East does, it is necessary to abandon this "classical" understanding of community as well as the "classical" starting point for explicating the Trinity.

Fortunately Bracken develops a new philosophical understanding of person and community. To begin with, person and community cannot be understood in isolation from each other. "To be a person is to belong to a community, i.e. a group of persons whose basis for association with one another is their recognition of each other as persons."[25] This community, when its unity is established simultaneously as a matter of free choice and yet as distinctively interpersonal, becomes a community in which responsibility to community and responsibility to person is equal. This means that person and community are strictly correlative concepts.

This understanding of community gives ontological status to the community and not only to the individual as in the "classical" approach. However, this ontological status does not mean that the community is a super-individual. This community is related to its larger context, but our concern now is the inner relations among the members of the community. This community is to be understood not as a static something but a community in which change is normative, in other words the community is a process as is the person and as is the whole of reality. Therefore a

---

[21] Ibid. 93.
[22] Ibid. 16.
[23] Ibid.
[24] Ibid.
[25] Ibid. 17.

redefinition of community is in order. "Community as process is a dynamic unity in totality of persons in continuous interaction with one another, who thereby constitute something bigger than themselves as separate
individuals, namely the community itself as a specifically social form of
process."[26]

This may sound more like the togetherness of three individual people,
each with a separate mind and will, going beyond what can be accepted
by an Eastern Christian. Bishop Kallistos explains that the distinction between the relations among the Trinity and the relations between three
people lies precisely at the point of mind and will. Whereas three people
would have three minds and three wills the Trinity is so intimately internally related one in the others that there is one mind and one will only. He
writes: "Father, Son and Spirit . . . have only one will and not three, only
one energy and not three. None of the three ever acts separately, apart from
the other two. They are not three Gods, but one God."[27] Actually Bracken
does go on to explain that "even though each divine person has his own
mind and will, they are of one mind and will in everything they say and
do, both with respect to one another and in their relationship with human
beings and the whole of creation."[28] For Bracken this community of divine
persons with one mind and will brought together out of three is, as in a
human community, a richer and deeper reality than would be one mind
alone.[29] I find the argument convincing. Whether an Eastern Christian
would think it sufficient I cannot be certain, but it seems consistent with
what Bishop Kallistos has said.

Bracken indicates that the community of the Trinity is so unified that
"they hold everything in common except the fact of their individual personhood, their relatedness to one another precisely as Father, Son and Holy
Spirit."[30] This certainly expounds a position shared by Eastern Christian
theologians. The East insists that even though the unity is complete it must
in no way confuse the distinction of the persons, "which is to be regarded
as an eternal distinction existing within the nature of God . . . Father, Son
and Spirit are not just 'modes' or 'moods' of the Divinity, not just masks
which God assumes for a time in his dealings with creation and then lays
aside. They are on the contrary three co-equal and co-eternal persons."[31]

---

[26] Ibid. 20.

[27] Timothy Ware (Bishop Kallistos), *The Orthodox Church* (New York: Penguin
Books, 1963) 37.

[28] Bracken, *The Triune Symbol* 26.

[29] Ibid.

[30] Ibid. 30.

[31] Ware, *The Orthodox Church* 38.

Bracken makes the same point, that the Trinity, while it is a unity, preserves at the same time the distinctiveness of the three persons. Both the unity and the distinctive persons are equally necessary. This explanation is specifically a matter of relationship. Therefore "if by some impossible supposition their relationship to one another were suspended they would cease to be, not only as a (divine) community, but also as individual persons."[32] Thus the person is dependent upon the community and the community is equally dependent upon the persons.

It is important from a process perspective that this Triune God not be an exception to reality as a whole, but rather be an exemplification of reality. Thus Bracken has begun with the human community that is mirrored in the Godhead. He develops this mirror image in Whiteheadian language as follows: "God is a structured society of three subsocieties. Each of the divine persons is a society of actual entities . . . which like the moments of temporal consciousness in human beings, rapidly succeed one another so as to produce the unified agency of the (divine) person. These three 'personally ordered' subsocieties, then, combine to produce the structured society which is their reality as one God. . . ."[33]

Granted that Thomas Hopko uses a different, non-Whiteheadian vocabulary, he is expressing the same point from an Eastern Christian perspective when he writes, "the interpersonal communion and relationship between creatures who are 'of one essence' really patterns . . . what exists perfectly and fully in an uncreated way in the Tri-personal Godhead. It is crucial because we claim that the Godhead is, in this important sense, *not* the great 'metaphysical exception,' but on the contrary, the metaphysical ground of creaturely, particularly human, being and life, both personal and communal; and that there are indeed real and perfect 'societal relationships' within the Godhead."[34] Thus both process theology and Eastern Christianity want to claim that God is not an exception but an exemplification of the whole of reality, albeit in a perfect way.

Another traditional doctrine that will need to be reinterpreted is the concept of human beings as created in the image of God. Given the process perspective thus far pictured, how can this image be interpreted and remain consistent with or at least be helpful in understanding the Eastern point of view? Bracken gives his answer as follows: "If God is . . . genuinely Triune, i.e. a community of three divine persons, then the image of God in creation cannot be *man* in the singular but only *man* as an ideal

[32] Bracken, *The Triune Symbol* 30.

[33] Ibid. 44.

[34] Thomas John Hopko, "God and the World: An Eastern Orthodox Response to Process Theology," Diss. Fordham University, 1982.

community of men and women who collectively represent the apex or climax of a world process. . . . Only the total Christ, Jesus together with all his brothers and sisters throughout history is the true image of the triune God."[35]

Since Gregory of Nyssa in the fourth century the Eastern tradition has used this doctrine and has interpreted it to mean that the image of God is reflected in all humanity, not in one individual. Hopko continues in this tradition, explaining how the East interprets the image of God. "This Eastern tradition further insists that the divinely perfect inter-personal relationship between the three divine hypostases has an analogy in the world and serves as the 'metaphysical archetype' for human inter-personal and societal relationships."[36] This is the reason Bishop Kallistos is able to say that a Christian cannot be a Christian alone, for to be a person is by definition to be internally related to other persons as the persons of the Trinity are eternally, internally related to each other.

Thus far Bracken has been helpful in his use of process terminology, thus showing the similarities between process theology and the Eastern tradition. Bracken does finally remain true to his Western heritage, however, in the way in which he describes the relationships within the Trinity itself. "They [Father, Son, and Spirit] constitute . . . the interpersonal process which is the divine life. The Father is the source of life and being within the Godhead communicating himself totally to the Son. The Son, in turn, responds perfectly to the initiative of the Father. The mediator between the Father and the Son, he who facilitates the exchange of life and love between them is the Spirit."[37]

The East would agree that the Father is "the source of life and being within the Godhead." Further they would agree that the Father "communicates himself totally to the Son," and that the Son responds. However, to have the Spirit be the "mediator" between the Father and the Son would cause an Eastern Christian to assume that the Spirit is now subordinate to the other two and so introduces a hierarchy into the structure, which is unacceptable. In the East the relationships are described in a way that avoids the possibility of hierarchy. Gregory of Nyssa offered an explanation. He wrote, "All that the Father is, we see revealed in the Son; all that is the Son's is the Father's also; for the whole Son dwells in the Father and he has the whole Father dwelling in himself. . . . The Son who exists always in the Father can never be separated from him, nor can the Spirit ever be divided from the Son who through the Spirit works all things. He who re-

---

[35] Bracken, *The Triune Symbol* 36.
[36] Hopko, "God and the World" 230.
[37] Bracken, *The Triune Symbol* 37, 38.

ceives the Father also receives at the same time the Son and the Spirit. It is impossible to envisage any kind of severance or disjunction between them."[38] These persons are so coinherent as to defy any kind of hierarchical structure, and the East argues that to be divine is sufficient. All of the divine persons are equal. There can be no degrees of divinity or hierarchy in the Trinity.

The final sentence of Bracken's description of the internal relationships of the Trinity shows that his description is definitely within the Western tradition as he speaks of the Spirit as the mediator between the Father and the Son. This disconnects the Trinity from its function of integrating salvation and christology and focuses on the Spirit's function within the Godhead to the exclusion of the Spirit's role in salvation. This is precisely the feature of Augustine's doctrine, followed by most other Western theologians, with which the East takes issue. This description of the Trinity would sound "classical" to Eastern ears because the Spirit has lost the distinction of his/her own personhood. "This doctrine of 'classical theism' is rejected by Orthodox theology of the Eastern Church on the basis that the Word and Spirit of God are revealed and known to be *persons* in Their own right, *acting* subjects who are other than who the Father is, essential to God's being to be sure, yet not defined in any way in which They lose the integrity of Their personal existence by being explained as parts, aspects, components, actions, instruments, or relations in and of God's innermost nature."[39] Bracken is most concerned to explain the internal relationships among the three persons of the Trinity. While the person/community concept is found as an analogy in the world there does not appear to be a direct correlation between the three persons of the Trinity and the saving work of God in creation. Here he seems closer to the tradition of Thomas Aquinas than to process thought.

Conclusion

Norman Pittenger's major contribution is in offering the worldview in which God is truly immanent in the world as the appropriate context for trinitarian theology. God is now in the world. Pittenger's Triunity is inadequate because he considers monotheism necessary to the Jewish-Christian tradition and fails to distinguish the three persons.

Lewis Ford adds the process understanding of the consequent nature of God, so now the world is in God. However, Ford's Logos is "actually deficient" and so inadequate to the actual presence of God in the world.

---

[38] Ware, *The Orthodox Church* 38, 39.
[39] Hopko, "God and the World" 206.

The Trinity developed by Joseph Bracken is compatible with the Eastern tradition in many respects. Both Bracken and the East begin with the community of the three persons and then move to the unity they embody as one God. Both also operate with the human community as an analogy to the divine community in the Godhead so that neither makes God a "metaphysical exception" over against the world but rather the "metaphysical archetype" of internal relatedness. Both Bracken and the East claim that in interpreting the idea of being created in the image of God, one must find the appropriate locus for the image not in an individual but in the community of the people of God.

The differences between the two interpretations of the Trinity are first that Bracken finally operates out of his Western tradition in describing the relations within the Godhead, and second that he does not relate these persons to the saving work of God in the world. Bracken appears to deny the integrity of the Third Person by making the Holy Spirit the "mediator/facilitator" between the Father and the Son. This is incompatible with Orthodoxy, since the distinctiveness of all three persons is definitely a priority in the Eastern tradition. Bracken is finally using the process concepts of person and community to create a doctrine of the Trinity that follows Augustine in denying the personhood of the third person of the Trinity by using this one to mediate between the other two. This use of the Spirit has been consistently encountered in the Western tradition, especially in those theologians who have intentionally followed Augustine.

It is, however, not necessary to follow Bracken to this final description of the Trinity. It is possible to continue the process development he has so ably begun by developing a doctrine of the Trinity that avoids both the Eastern critique of monotheism and the Western concern about tritheism. The affinities between process thought and the Eastern tradition are striking: the worldview of interconnectedness, the immanence of God in the world, the understanding of persons and community as being necessary to each other, and the insistence that God not be a metaphysical exception. Process theology should develop its own trinitarian doctrine in relation to the Eastern tradition with which it shares so many basic understandings. A primary concern should be to include the Eastern insistence that the function of the doctrine of the Trinity is to integrate christology and soteriology in a doctrine of God.

Chapter Eight

A Reauthenticated Doctrine of the Trinity

In order to develop a reauthenticated doctrine of the Trinity we need to draw upon the contributions of the above resources. Thus a brief review of the specific contributions provided by each group or person is in order.

Contributions from Eastern Orthodox Christianity

The primary contribution of the Eastern tradition is the understanding that the purpose of the doctrine of the Trinity is to integrate the concepts of salvation, Christ, and God in a way that summarizes the theology of this tradition. Thus the Trinity as Father, Son, and Holy Spirit is indicative of an understanding of salvation for which the paradigm is transfiguration. As Jesus was transfigured on Mount Tabor, so all people and by extension the world have the potential for that same experience. This is possible because we are created in the image of God, which means that what defines us as human is our internal relationship with God. It also means that the task we are invited to undertake is to realize that image by revealing God's love for the world through our own words and deeds. This gradual process of our becoming God by God's grace contributes to the salvation of the world around us. We are the leaven in the loaf. This understanding of salvation points to God's persuasive manner of relating to the world in order to accomplish salvation.

Jesus is identified as Son in order to indicate the close connection between him and the Father so that what is revealed in the Son is trustworthy. This Christ of God is again the leaven in the loaf. In this case, because Christ is both truly God and truly human, humanity is transfigured by the presence of the divinity in the humanity. Moreover, this Son provides the understanding of the goal of humanity, becoming God. While the Son is God by nature, we will become God by grace.

As the Father is present within the world and as the Son is present in the person called Jesus, so the Holy Spirit is present within each believer providing faith and perseverance to follow the Way of God, making it possible for all baptized people to achieve *theosis,* that is, to become God by grace. In that process the salvation of the world is brought about. Thus this Trinity of Father, Son, and Holy Spirit is necessary, and necessary in these categories in order for salvation to occur in this way. This Eastern Trinity provides a pattern to follow in integrating salvation, christology, and God into a summary formula.

Contributions from Augustine and the West

The primary contribution of Augustine is his concern for the oneness of God and his fear that to speak of three persons runs the risk of meaning three gods. His emphasis on the oneness as the divine simplicity shows us what happens when the doctrine of the Trinity is separated from the concepts of christology and salvation, and thus fails in its original function. It becomes abstract and appears to be a riddle that requires explanation rather than a shorthand description of an entire theology.

This happens because Augustine develops a very different understanding of salvation in which "becoming like God" is a description of sin at its worst, and salvation is described as being elected by God. This happens because God in the East is persuasively related to the world while for Augustine God in relation to the world is all-powerful in such a way that God's grace is irresistible. Augustine's system begins with the creation of the soul, which falls into the world and suffers. Only if God is gracious to that soul will it again rise to the presence of God for eternity. Salvation is limited to human beings. The world does not participate except as a stage for the drama of human salvation. Salvation is limited to those human beings who are elected by God, with the rest of humanity being lost. This is just and right because all human beings are guilty of original sin, which is passed on by fathers to their children, so that all people deserve punishment. Only because God is merciful will anyone be saved. The manner of God's relation to the world is no longer persuasive, but coercive and predetermined, for the grace of God according to Augustine is both separated from our human nature and irresistible, and the decision for election is made by God before the creation of the world.

Jesus the Christ becomes the solution to the problem of original sin, which Augustine locates in our sexuality. The Christ comes to undo the damage done by the fall as described in Genesis 3. Thus it is necessary for Jesus to die the death of a criminal in order to be the fitting sacrifice for human sin. It is also necessary that he rise again to live with God. Only thus can we see that overcoming sin and death is possible for God.

Since even the grace of God is external to us in this view the presence of the Holy Spirit of God within us is out of the question. The Holy Spirit's function is to be the love that holds the Father and the Son together within the Trinity.

Augustine is operating with a received doctrine of the Trinity that does not fit with his understanding of salvation, Christ, or God. He is also indebted to the Christian tradition for the understanding that there is one God. His doctrine emphasizes this oneness in that he develops the divine simplicity that is behind the Trinity in order to insure that God is one. He does this because the Eastern Christian theologians who developed the Trinitarian doctrine based on three distinct but not separate *hypostases* seemed to him to compromise the oneness of God. Augustine does clearly reflect a Western concern that the Eastern Trinity sounds too much like three Gods, which would be against the tradition of God as one. In his concern to maintain the oneness of God his doctrine of the Trinity becomes abstract and its relationship to the rest of Christian theology becomes obscure.

Luther and Calvin

During the course of the Reformation Luther and Calvin both acknowledged the doctrine of the Trinity and both spoke of salvation in terms of election. Although Calvin is traditionally noted for the doctrine of predestination, Luther was also logically driven to this conclusion. Both also focused the action of God in the world on Jesus so that much of Protestant theology can be described as christocentric. Salvation continues to be centered on human beings to the exclusion of the rest of the world, and humanity is divided into those who are elected and those who are not. Thus these figures of the Reformation, like Augustine, were influenced by the move toward individualism in their understanding of salvation. While both theologians use the doctrine of the Trinity as the organizing principle, following the Apostle's Creed, neither one makes explicitly clear how this doctrine undergirds or is related to the doctrines of Christ and salvation.

Recent Western Theologians

Recent Western theologians have followed Augustine, Luther, and Calvin in their development of the Trinity. To this has been added a focus on Jesus as the only presence of God in the world, which confines the Holy Spirit to the relationship between the Father and the Son in the Godhead. Thus the tendency toward monotheism is strong enough to overwhelm an authentic doctrine of the Trinity. The exceptions noted here are Cyril Richardson, who abandons the doctrine of the Trinity altogether, Leonard Hodgson, Henry P. Van Dusen, and Jürgen Moltmann. Moltmann is most critical of this Western monotheism. He acknowledges his indebtedness to the Eastern tradition in his effort to develop a Trinity that is able to maintain the distinctions of the three persons. He is especially concerned that the Holy Spirit be equal to the others as a person. The unity (not oneness) is achieved by means of *perichoresis* or coinherence, which is weak without a metaphysic to explain how this coinherence is possible. Moltmann is still in the process of working out the ramifications of this doctrine for the rest of his theology, but he does appreciate that this doctrine is where soteriology and christology converge into a doctrine of God.

Contributions from Feminism

Feminist theology has reminded us that the way of God in the world is persuasive, that we are created in the image of God and so are intended to be part of the process of salvation. Feminism has opened our eyes to the fact that our images of God are limited and limiting and have historically been used to exclude women from leadership roles in the Church. Much of what feminists write is rightly critical of the Augustinian way of doing theology, so there is an understanding of salvation that emphasizes interrelatedness, cooperation between God and human beings, and salvation as something that occurs here and now and includes the whole creation. In approaching christology feminists emphasize the Christ as the presence of God in the world in a way that is not limited to Jesus, although that presence is surely to be seen in him. This makes it possible to include women as well as men as persons in whom God is present. The relationship between God and persons is not one of power-over or judgment, but one of friendship and cooperation. The goal is not to control others but to free them to respond to God as they are able.

In re-imaging how God works in the world feminists draw upon women's experience of God and of the world and of God in the world, and so are also re-imaging God in an effort to find language that does not exclude women from identifying with God. Thus Sallie McFague suggests a Trinity of Mother, Lover, and Friend that renews language, as does Elizabeth Johnson who develops a Trinity of Sophia-Spirit, Sophia-Christ, and Sophia-Mother. Each of these Trinities is an attempt to explain a received doctrine rather than to develop a feminist theology and to see if the Trinity, renamed, can integrate christology and salvation into a doctrine of

God. The challenge of Christian feminism is to develop a comprehensive theology and a vocabulary that includes women.

It is significant to note that the feminist view of the world has much in common with the Eastern Christian understanding: salvation occurs here as well as in the future, and is a process of transformation from the world as we know it into the world alive with God. Salvation involves the whole world because everything is interrelated with everything else. Human beings are created in the image of God and related to God in a way that makes synergy or cooperation possible and desirable. Sin is not participating in the process of salvation and thus refusing to enter into relationship with God. Sin is both against God and against the world. Christ is the evidence of transfiguration or transformation, and God is relating to the world in a way that is persuasive.

Contributions from Process Thought

The process theologians reviewed in chapter 7 agree with feminists, particularly Sallie McFague, that the context for Trinitarian theology is panentheistic. They also add their own understanding of God as distinct in two natures, the Primordial Nature and the Consequent Nature, and they provide the philosophical clarification to understand the coinherence of the natures of God.

A reauthenticated Trinity will integrate salvation and christology and a doctrine of God into a Trinity that relates to the world in a way that is always in the process of saving the world. The next section will describe salvation, christology, and God from the perspective of process theology.

The Trinity Reauthenticated

From a process perspective salvation is an ongoing, persuasive, reciprocal process between God and the world that results in harmony in God and harmony in the world. Salvation depends upon the persuasive agency of God to involve people in participating in this process. Since salvation includes the cosmos there is no human endeavor that can be outside of, not engaged in, or unnecessary to salvation. Thus salvation, which can also be described as the transformation of the world from its current situation into one that is harmonious, can only come about by human agency cooperating with the attractiveness of God who lures us into a salvific vision of the future.

This process is reciprocal in that God provides possible futures from which we choose one, thus rejecting the others. In response to this choice God then provides a new set of possible futures from which choices are again made. If the choices enhance harmony God and the world rejoice. If the choices result in discord God reconciles all that is possible and submits the reconciled results to the world. In this view it is possible to have suffering in God as well as in the world because God experiences what we experience, only with greater intensity.

The conception of all this as possible is based upon a process view of the world that locates God's involvement at the most basic level, which is a unit, an indivisible event. Whitehead named these events "actual entities" or "actual occasions." Each event includes in itself its history of past actual occasions. This is called its "physical pole" because it gives rise to what we ordinarily think of as the physical world. Each actual entity entertains alternative possibilities for its own actualization. The aspect of God from which these derive is called the Primordial Nature. The immanence of these possibilities in the actual entity is called the "mental pole." This actual entity then creatively constitutes itself by integrating its physical pole and its mental pole. This completed actual entity then participates in constituting the physical pole of future actual entities. It is a process that proceeds from the past into the future. (See Figure 1 on following page.)

This worldview understands the power of the past to influence the new occasions, but it also views change as inevitable because novelty is also included in the composition of each actual occasion. Novelty comes to the entity as a lure into the particular future for that occasion. The occasion freely responds to this lure, accepting or rejecting it. This implies that freedom and change are both located at the most fundamental level of the universe. Since it is God's primordial nature whose immanence constitutes the lure into the future for each actual occasion, God is also immanent in the world at this fundamental level, and not only when the universe reaches the complexity of human beings.

Process thought is designed primarily to explain how the whole universe works and functions in relation to God at the most basic level, but it also describes the more complicated way things function at the level of complexity reached in human persons. Persons are analyzed as "personally ordered societies." A "society" is a collection of intimately interacting actual occasions. A person is a society in which there is only one member at a time, with a flow into each occasion of the preceding ones. This person or flow of personal experience is non-substantial. There is no concrete thing that is you or me. "There is no fixed entity or aspect of human experience that is uniformly designated by 'I.' . . . The one who says 'I' refers to the ultimate subject of conscious experience and the ultimate agent of responsible action."[1]

---

[1] John B. Cobb, Jr., *Christ in a Pluralistic Age* (Philadelphia: Westminster, 1975) 123.

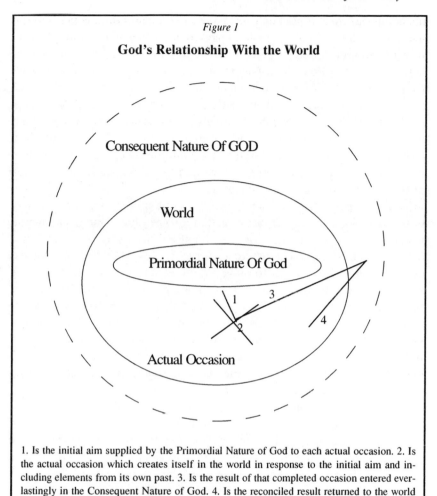

Figure 1

God's Relationship With the World

1. Is the initial aim supplied by the Primordial Nature of God to each actual occasion. 2. Is the actual occasion which creates itself in the world in response to the initial aim and including elements from its own past. 3. Is the result of that completed occasion entered everlastingly in the Consequent Nature of God. 4. Is the reconciled result returned to the world which Whitehead calls the kingdom of God and I have called Christ. This also shows how it is that God is in the world and the world is in God.

Each occasion of personal life is constituted by a physical pole and a mental pole, as are all actual occasions. The physical pole includes everything that influences us from our past. Since we are so very heavily influenced by our past we perceive ourselves to be more substantial than we really are. This also encourages us to think of our world as made up of substantial things, and it encourages us to view the world as stable and unchanging. Whitehead argues that, like the world around and within us, we are constantly changing, even though usually those changes are imperceptible from moment to moment. We speak of growing up and growing old, acknowledging the changes that do occur. The change that is introduced occurs in our mental pole as we choose to accept some new possibilities and reject others. We thus create ourselves anew moment by moment.

We have seen that our choice is made possible by a "lure for feeling" derived from the Primordial Nature of God. Whether it is realized or rejected, what we become is incorporated into God. This aspect of God, God as including the world, is called the Consequent Nature of God. What happens in the Consequent Nature in turn affects the world. The difference between human beings and simple entities is that we are of sufficient complexity to comprehend that in fact the lure into the future is from God and to understand that we have the freedom to participate in the salvation of the world or to inhibit that salvation.

Since our participation is a major part of this process we are necessary to the salvation not only of ourselves but also of others and of the world. It is possible for us to ignore or intentionally move away from the vision or direction of God so that the process of salvation is blocked. We possess the freedom and the power to move in opposition to God's transforming vision for the future. God honors our human freedom and risks human power because the potential for good and the potential for evil rise together. The role of the persuasive agency of God in the world is to convince people to work for harmony and against discord. Since this agency is persuasive and not coercive there is no guarantee that harmony will overcome discord in the world. Salvation is not something that God does to us or for us but something that we and God do together. We assume the risk together. Salvation for us then is both a grand invitation to a harmonious future and an awesome responsibility because it depends on us. In this view the response we have to make is not a token but a great task. This is lived out in response to the living God who is leading us into the future.

Clearly, since we bear much responsibility for the salvation of the world the process assessment of what is possible for human beings is much more positive than the assessment of humans by classical Protestant theology. The idea of human beings as totally depraved is not accepted by process thought. Human beings are the most complex organisms in the world, and this makes us capable of the greatest good and the greatest evil. The destructive capability of persons is taken seriously in process thought but it does not define who we are as human beings. Our definition comes from our potentiality for cooperation with God in a way that will benefit the whole world. The connection with Orthodoxy—creation in the image of God—as well as McFague's use of this same concept in a feminist framework indicate that understanding ourselves in relation to God in a positive way is part of the oldest Christian tradition and also a rediscovery for women and process theologians.

Salvation for human beings involves recognizing our interrelationship with all other species and our environment. Salvation from a process perspective will include all creation, so that the harmonizing required for salvation relates to all species and the whole environment. Because we are the most complex creatures and exert the greatest influence over what happens to the rest of the world, how we choose to exercise our power will either support the possibility of salvation for all or thwart it. This inclusive scope for salvation again comes out of the ancient tradition of Christianity in which we are the agents of God who bring about the transfiguration of the world. The vocabulary is different but the concept is the same. This understanding of salvation is also consistent with feminist concerns, especially with those of the eco-feminists, who interpret salvation as healing for all people and for the world as well.

God, as understood by Whitehead, has the same bipolar structure as all other actual entities. God has both a "mental pole" and a "physical pole." While for human beings and the rest of the created world the "physical pole" comes first, for God the "mental pole" is the beginning of God's actuality, so that God is the origin of creativity and novelty.

The doctrine of God developed by Whitehead primarily in *Process and Reality* is also a description of who God is in terms of how God relates to the world. Whitehead chose to develop his own vocabulary. The term Primordial Nature is used to describe the "mental pole" of God, the one who is "free, complete, primordial, eternal, actually deficient, and unconscious."[2] This nature of God is free and eternal because it is unconditioned by the rest of reality. It is complete in that it includes all pure possibilities, realizing the unlimitedness of potentiality. This nature is primordial because it is presupposed by all temporal realities. It is eternal because it is independent of time and unaffected by temporal events. It is actually deficient because it is only one pole of God, the conceptual one, whereas actuality is attained only physically. It is this nature of God that provides the vision of possibilities for the world or the lure for feeling that moves the world toward greater freedom and greater harmony.

Whitehead uses the term Consequent Nature to describe the reality of God that is "determined, incomplete, consequent, 'everlasting,' fully actual, and conscious."[3] This nature is determined because it is conditioned by the reality of the world. This is the "physical pole" of God that incorporates the world by feeling all of its feelings. It is incomplete because there are always new events in the world to be incorporated and integrated

[2] Alfred North Whitehead, *Process and Reality,* ed. David R. Griffin and Donald W. Sherburne (New York: The Free Press, 1978) 210.

[3] Ibid. 345.

with the old. It is consequent in that it derives its experience from the world, which it takes into itself, and it is thus dependent upon both the primordial nature and the world. It is everlasting because although it relates to the temporal passage it has no beginning and no end. It is fully actual because it weaves the physical feelings of the world into the mental pole and thus constitutes the actual entity that is God. It is conscious because it has in eminent degree that complexity of integration of the physical and mental that is required for consciousness to arise. "The consequent nature of God is his judgment on the world. He saves the world as it passes into the immediacy of his own life. It is the judgment of a tenderness which loses nothing that can be saved."[4] After saving the world and perfecting it the Consequent Nature passes the perfected actuality back into the temporal world, which has the effect of creating the Reign of God in the world. "What is done in the world is transformed into a reality in heaven, and the reality in heaven passes back into the world. By reason of this reciprocal relation, the love in the world passes into the love in heaven, and floods back again into the world. In this sense, God is the great companion—the fellow sufferer who understands."[5]

The relationship between God and the world is reciprocal and thus infinitely repeated. The Primordial Nature provides the lure for feeling for every actual occasion, which then responds more or less positively or negatively to this lure. Since this response is free, freedom is located at this basic level of the world. Regardless of the outcome, the result is taken up into the Consequent Nature, passing into the immediacy of God and finally again flowing into the world. The relationship between God and the world brings about change in God in the Consequent Nature, which in turn brings about change in the world. This cycle of events describes a relationship between God and the world that is salvific. In order for the world to exist, God is necessary. In order for the world to be transfigured, it must incarnate God. Whitehead has created an understanding of salvation and a doctrine of God that are highly integrated. The task that remains for Christian theologians is to develop a christology that is consistent with this understanding of God and the world and also consistent with the Christian tradition.

The understanding in the Christian tradition of who Jesus is as the Christ is pluralistic from the very beginning. The Christ who is portrayed as a prophet like Moses in the gospel of Matthew is different from the Christ of the gospel of John who is high and lifted up and in control of everything that happens. These both differ from the crucified Messiah of the gospel of

---

[4] Ibid. 346.
[5] Ibid. 351.

Mark. All these are attempts to describe who this person is who is identified by his followers as the Christ/Messiah and then to interpret what his being the Christ meant for the ones who chose to follow in the way.

The earliest divisions in the Church came about because of differences in the interpretations of Jesus Christ and how he is/was related to God. The dispute between Arius and Athanasius is but one example. The two primary ways that developed for doing christology were represented by the theological schools in Alexandria and Antioch. Both were driven by the concern to understand salvation as a reality. Theologians from Antioch began with the humanity of Jesus, since if he is not truly human then humans are not the objects of salvation. Out of the same concern theologians in Alexandria began with the Logos-Son of God who becomes human, in order to insure that he has the divine power needed to save humanity. Both groups agreed that it was necessary for Jesus Christ to be truly divine and truly human at the same time in order for salvation to be achieved.

It is possible from a process perspective to address these concerns because of the process understanding of salvation and the process understanding of God. One process response to the issue of christology is developed in John Cobb's *Christ in a Pluralistic Age*. Cobb identifies the Primordial Nature of God with the Logos who "is an eternal aspect of deity transcending every actual world as the principle of possibility and of the relevance of that possibility."[6] This Logos is immanent in the world in all actual occasions as their initial aim, which is the energy moving toward actualization. To the degree that this aim is realized the new occasion is something more than the mere outgrowth of the past, and thus creative transformation occurs. Human beings resist this call to be transformed, clinging to the security of past ways. We usually experience God's presence in us as something alien—sometimes judging, sometimes challenging, sometimes strengthening, sometimes healing. In Jesus this immanence of God was at times fully integrated with his own selfhood, so that his person was co-constituted by his own human past and the present activity of God. In this way his very self was creatively transformed by God.

Jesus' message opened others to God's transformative power and continues to do so today. Also his life, death, and resurrection appearances generated a powerful field of force. Those who are incorporated into this field are further opened to God's creative transformation of their lives. This creative transformation, incarnate in Jesus' selfhood, supported by Jesus' teaching, and strengthened by his historical impact, is Christ. Christ is present everywhere. Jesus *is* the Christ.

---

[6] Cobb, *Christ in a Pluralistic Age* 77.

Cobb develops his process christology in a way that identifies Christ with the initial aim of the Primordial Nature of God. I would propose a different approach in developing a process christology. Christ is the initial instance of the causal efficacy of the kingdom of heaven in the world. Whitehead describes four creative phases the universe must experience in order to be actualized. The first phase can be identified as the Primordial Nature of God. It is "the phase of conceptual origination, deficient in actuality, but infinite in its adjustment of valuation."[7] This phase is the source of the vision and lures for feeling for the world. The world is the second or "temporal phase of physical origination, with its multiplicity of actualities. In this phase full actuality is attained."[8] The third phase is identified with the Consequent Nature of God and is "the phase of perfected actuality."[9] Whitehead calls the fourth phase the kingdom of heaven. It is here that creative action is completed. "For the perfected actuality passes back into the temporal world, and qualifies this world so that each temporal actuality includes it as an immediate fact of relevant experience."[10]

This perspective applied to christology results in a Jesus who is born in the temporal world (phase two). In each instant of his life he accepted the lure for feeling offered by the Primordial Nature of God for his life, even though sometimes he accepted only after prayerful consideration, hoping it could be different. His acceptance of this lure is perfected in the Consequent Nature of God (phase three) and passes back into the temporal world (phase four) so that people respond to Jesus as the Christ of God, as the presence of God actualized in the world. Thus Jesus becomes the Christ by accepting the lures of God, by being perfected by God and by being recognized as the presence of God in the world. Thus in Jesus as the Christ the reign of God is at hand, as the gospel of Mark says. In Christ the Jesus who accepts the initial aims is joined with the perfected aims that have been given to the world by the Consequent Nature so that the presence of God is actualized in the world and the cycle is complete. The primary difference between this view and the views of Cobb and Ford, who locate Christ in the initial aim, is the inclusion of the actual perfected presence of God in the world in the concept of Christ. Thus in this perspective Christ is where phase two and phase four come together so that the salvation that is begun by Christ is actualized in the world. This is necessary in order for God to be actualized in the world in a way that is recognizable so as to account for the recognition by the early Christians that God was

[7] Whitehead, *Process and Reality* 350.
[8] Ibid. 350.
[9] Ibid.
[10] Ibid. 351.

in Christ. It also indicates that Christ is necessary to the creative and saving process that is the activity of God in relation to the world.

This perspective makes it possible for us to identify with Jesus, who is truly human and points out for us how it is possible for us to become God. We, like Jesus, have the possibility of accepting the lures of feeling given to us by the Primordial Nature of God. Since we will not accept all the lures we will sometimes experience this presence as judging; thus we will not become God as Jesus did but we will be transfigured when we accept the lure and we will contribute to the transformation of the world into the Reign of God and thus to renewing the presence of Christ in the world. As we follow the example of Jesus by accepting the lures of God we are also being perfected by the Consequent Nature of God and our actions are passed back into the world. Since we do not accept every lure for feeling as Jesus did we will not become God or reach perfection until we live everlastingly in the Consequent Nature of God. But our contributions of transformation will remain everlastingly in the Consequent Nature of God and will be passed back into the world, renewing Christ's presence, building up the reign of God, and participating in the transformation of the whole world.

Now that all three theological pieces are gathered, namely a process understanding of salvation, a process understanding of God, and a process understanding of Christ, it remains to be seen how a Trinity can be developed that is able to integrate all three.

In order for this Trinity to be reauthenticated it will perform the same function as the original Trinity did. It will be appropriate to our current context and will require the action of the whole Trinity together in order to bring about the salvation of the world.

For a process Trinity to be true to its own tradition it must take time seriously so that while this explication of a process Trinity is appropriate to the current context, when the context changes—and it will—it will be necessary to reconfigure or at least to rename this doctrine in order for it to be appropriate to the new context. For the same reason this process Trinity cannot simply use the vocabulary of an earlier era, although some continuity helps to hold the Christian tradition together. Whereas Father, Son, and Holy Spirit were appropriate Trinitarian designations for Athanasius and the Eastern Christian tradition, enabling them to integrate their understandings of salvation, Christ, and God in the philosophical language and based on the scriptural interpretation common at that time, a Trinity based in process thought must integrate a quite different non-substantial philosophy and a worldview that reflects this commitment. It must also reflect the current context in which linguistic concerns raised by feminists and the current status of scriptural interpretation play a major role. Now that we are aware of the male bias of the Greek language and of most philosophy, we can appreciate that most of the language of Scripture also reflects this patriarchal worldview. Thus we are not surprised that all language about God is male language. Since we now have a new context as well as a different philosophical understanding, the language of Father, Son, and Holy Spirit is no longer adequate to this time and place.

In order for a process Trinity to be faithful to the tradition it must integrate a process understanding of salvation, christology, and God as the original Trinity also integrated these three doctrines.

There are three *hypostases* in this Trinity. Each *hypostasis* is differentiated from the others by the specific role it plays in the salvation of the world. The first *hypostasis* of this Trinity is the Primordial Nature of God, which provides the lure for feeling, the initial aim, to each and every actual occasion. The occasion then either appropriates or rejects this lure and the results are then taken up into the Consequent Nature, the second *hypostasis*. In this nature God redeems the actual occasion and saves it everlastingly. The world is then influenced by what this occasion has become in God. This influence in the world is the reign of God. It is in the Christ, the third *hypostasis,* and the initial and supreme concretion of this reign of heaven, that salvation is encountered and made known to us. In a process context the integration of these three *hypostases* exists in the concretion of every actual occasion and thus at the most basic level of existence. Nothing can come into existence and participate in salvation without the coinherence of the actions of the three *hypostases* of the Trinity. By the same token everything that comes into existence will have the possibility of participating in the salvation of the world.

In order to remain consistent with the process vocabulary the possible language for a process Trinity would include Primordial Nature, Consequent Nature, and Christ. I propose to use the term Lover for the Primordial Nature of God. This term has the advantage of being the noun that names what the Christian tradition has most often proclaimed about God, i.e., that God is love. It is also definitely a relational term, and relationship is emphasized in process theology. In addition it is gender neutral which is important in our current context. In considering this term I appreciate McFague's insistence that God's love for the world is not passionless, so that when we say "God so loved the world" this is not intended to be a disinterested, passionless love for which the world is not necessary; rather, in accordance with the process perspective, God's relationship to the world is necessary if God is to be actualized at all. God is identified with the future of the world, the Consequent Nature of God, and therefore God is passionately interested in the harmonious future of the world.

The term for the Consequent Nature of God is Spirit. This follows from the function of the Consequent Nature and its parallel to the function of the Spirit in the original Trinity. It is in the Consequent Nature of God that the world is taken up constantly, transformed, and retained everlastingly. In the Trinity of the East it is the Holy Spirit who receives the believers who have been transfigured and who at death continue this journey in the Spirit until transfiguration is complete. While the Consequent Nature is broader in scope, including the whole world rather than only human persons, the Spirit is in both cases the locus of everlastingness. This term has the advantage of being part of the Christian tradition and yet nonspecific enough to be redefined in terms of the Consequent Nature of God.

The final *hypostasis* of the Trinity is the Christ. The Christ is that aspect of the Consequent Nature that passes back into the world to actualize the reign of God and to provide us with the knowledge of who God is and how God relates to the world in combination with the initial aims that are offered to each actual occasion by the Primordial Nature of God. It would be possible not to have this aspect of the Consequent Nature, but this would mean that whatever salvation or change occurs would only occur in God and would never have any effect on the world. Thus in order to embody a process understanding of salvation as something that occurs here and now it is necessary to include this third *hypostasis*. The Christ is that aspect of God who actualizes salvation in the world. From the perspective of the Christian tradition Christ also is the preferred term, because not only does it name the event of the coming of the reign of God in the world, it is the name that those who follow in this tradition choose to be identified by: that is, we are Christians. Given our context it is significant that this term, like the others, is gender neutral, at least in the English language.

Speaking of God as personal and so anthropomorphizing God helps people focus on the relationship between God and human beings. This we have done in the discussion of christology. But in the Christian tradition this focus has been at considerable expense to the rest of the world. Whitehead intentionally relates God to the world at the sub-atomic level to indicate that God pervades the whole world and also to portray salvation as a world-encompassing event and not only an experience for human beings. For addressing the current ecological crisis it is appropriate that this process Trinity be both relational to human beings who have the power to change themselves and the world and relational to the world at its fundamental level. Thus Lover, Christ, and Spirit are all *hypostases* of God—differentiated by their respective roles in the on-going creation/salvation of the world, but united in that very act of salvation that occurs at the fundamental level of the actualization of every actual occasion in the universe.

This Trinity is united in its loving purpose of creating and saving the world, which are the beginning and end of a single process. It is united also in the Spirit who contains the Lover and the Christ as well as the whole of the universe. This Trinity addresses the concern that God is one, since God is one actual occasion. God is also a unity in the same way that all other actual occasions are unities. The only exception is that in God the mental pole begins the process, adding the physical pole and creatively combining the two to achieve actuality, i.e., to become concrete. The instant in which this process occurs is so minute that this Trinity comes into being simultaneously. One can speak of source or cause or time in relation to how the Trinity relates to the world, but again the time involved is instantaneous. Nevertheless it is possible to say that the Lover who provides the lure for salvation to the actual occasion begins the cycle. This initial aim is the presence of Christ in the world but only potentially, since at this point it could be rejected. The Spirit receives the creative construction made by the actual occasion of itself, transforming it and returning this contribution to the reign of God in the actuality that is the Christ. This Christ who is the actuality of the reign of God in the world also remains everlastingly in the Spirit. Then the Spirit communicates the changed context to the Lover who provides the initial aim, the best possible lure, for the next actual occasion. And the process continues, bringing about the salvation of the world.

This process doctrine of the Trinity can begin with either the three or the one and it will result in the same formulation. Whether the process begins with God as Actual Occasion or God as Lover, Christ, and Spirit, the relationships will remain and the resultant salvation will be the same. I began with the three in order to emphasize the necessity of each of the three *hypostases* in the process of salvation and to be clear that this is not a typical Western formulation of the doctrine. Another difference includes the relationships among the three *hypostases*. It is the Spirit that contains the other two and it is not possible to speak of origin since all come into being simultaneously such that all three are necessary for an actual occasion to be actualized. Thus the distinctions and relationships are not described by means of origin and relationship to one of the three. In this process Trinity it is possible to describe Christ as the result of the actions of both the Lover and the Spirit. The Lover initiates the aim, the Spirit reconciles the response to that aim and returns the reconciled response, Christ, to the world, making God actually present in the world in a saving way. The Lover relies on the communication from the Spirit as to the result of the previous initial aim in order to provide an appropriate next initial aim. The Spirit reconciles all responses and retains them everlastingly as well as communicating the reconciled response to the Lover and incarnating that response by means of the Christ in the world. All three *hypostases* are necessary for salvation to be actualized, and they are necessary in the manner described. Because of the clarity of the distinctions between the *hypostases* in this Trinity it cannot be collapsed into a simple oneness. Because of the necessary interrelatedness of the three this Trinity does not exhibit tritheism. Thus the doctrine of the Trinity now, once again, performs its original function of integrating christology and salvation into a doctrine of God who is a Trinity. It also reinstates the paradox of God as a unity and God as three, but does so in such a way that the paradox cannot be resolved without losing the salvation of the world.

This reauthenticated Trinity of Lover, Christ, and Spirit is clearly linked to the Christian tradition in its integration of salvation and christology in a trinitarian doctrine of God. It also integrates the process understandings of God, salvation, and Christ so that God's saving relationship is with the whole world and at its fundamental level as well as at the level of human experience. Finally, the theology and language of this Trinity is most appropriate to the context in which God and the world live. Thus the Trinity has been reauthenticated.

Bibliography

Althaus, Paul. *The Theology of Martin Luther.* Translated by Robert C. Schultz. Philadelphia: Fortress, 1981.

Aristotle. *The Ten Categories on Interpretation.* Translated by H. P. Cooke. Cambridge, Mass.: Harvard University Press, 1967.

Augustine. *The City of God.* Translated by Gerald Walsh; edited by Vernon Bourke. New York: Doubleday, 1958.

_____. *On Christian Doctrine.* Translated by D. W. Robertson, Jr. Indianapolis: Bobbs-Merrill, 1984.

_____. *On Free Choice of the Will.* Translated by Anna S. Benjamin and L. H. Hackstaff. Indianapolis: Bobbs-Merrill, 1984.

_____. *The Trinity.* Translated by Stephen McKenna. Washington, D.C.: Catholic University of America Press, 1963.

Barth, Karl. *Church Dogmatics.* Translated by G. W. Bromiley. New York: Harper and Row, 1961.

_____. *Church Dogmatics* I.1. New York: Charles Scribner's Sons, 1969.

_____. *Dogmatics in Outline.* Translated by G. T. Thomson. New York: Harper and Row, 1959.

_____. *Credo.* New York: Charles Scribner's Sons, 1962.

Basil the Great. *On the Holy Spirit.* Crestwood, N.Y.: St. Vladimir's Seminary Press, 1980.

Battenhouse, Roy W. *A Companion to the Study of St. Augustine.* Grand Rapids: Baker Book House, 1979.

The Book of Concord. The Confessions of the Evangelical Lutheran Church. Translated and edited by Theodore G. Tappert in collaboration with Jaroslav Pelikan, Robert H. Fischer [and] Arthur C. Piepkorn. Philadelphia: Muhlenberg Press, 1959.

Bracken, Joseph A. *The Triune Symbol: Persons, Process, and Community.* New York: University Press of America, 1985.

Brown, Peter. *Augustine of Hippo.* Berkeley: University of California Press, 1969.

Burleigh, J. H. S., ed. *Augustine: Earlier Works.* Philadelphia: Westminster, 1953.

Burnaby, John, ed. *Augustine: Later Works.* Philadelphia: Westminster, 1955.

Chadwick, Henry. *The Early Church.* The Pelican History of the Church, ed. Owen Chadwick. New York: Penguin Books, 1983.

Cobb, John B. *Christ in a Pluralistic Age.* Philadelphia: Westminster, 1975.

Davies, J. G. *The Early Christian Church.* Grand Rapids: Baker Book House, 1989.

Every, George. *Misunderstandings Between East and West.* Richmond, Va.: John Knox, 1966.

Frend, W. H. C. *The Rise of Christianity.* Philadelphia: Fortress, 1989.

Ford, Lewis. *The Lure of God.* Philadelphia: Fortress, 1978.

Geanakopolos, Deno John. *Byzantine East and Latin West.* Oxford: Blackwell, 1966.

Gregg, Robert C., and Dennis Groh. *Early Arianism—a View of Salvation.* Philadelphia: Fortress, 1981.

Gritsch, Eric W. *Martin—God's Court Jester.* Philadelphia: Fortress, 1983.

Hall, Stuart G. *Doctrine and Practice in the Early Church.* Grand Rapids: Eerdmans, 1991.

Hodgson, Leonard. *The Doctrine of the Trinity.* New York: Charles Scribner's Sons, 1944.

Hopko, Thomas J. "God and the World: An Eastern Orthodox Response to Process Theology." Fordham University, 1982.

Jenson, Robert. *The Triune Identity: God according to the Gospel.* Philadelphia: Fortress, 1982.

Johnson, Elizabeth. *She Who Is: The Mystery of God in Feminist Theological Discourse.* New York: Crossroad, 1993.

Jüngel, Eberhard. *The Doctrine of the Trinity.* Translated by Horton Harris. Edinburgh: Scottish Academic Press, 1976.

Kelly, J. N. D. *Early Christian Creeds.* New York: McKay, 1972.

_____. *Early Christian Doctrines.* San Francisco: Harper and Row, 1960.

Kerr, Hugh T. *A Compend of The Institutes of the Christian Religion by John Calvin.* Philadelphia: Westminster, 1964.

Lossky, Vladimir. *In the Image and Likeness of God.* Edited by John H. Erickson and Thomas E. Bird. New York: St. Vladimir's Seminary Press, 1974.

Luther, Martin. *Luther's Works.* Vol. 24. Edited by Jaroslav Pelikan. Philadelphia: Fortress, 1975.

McFague, Sallie. *Models of God.* Philadelphia: Fortress, 1987.

_____. *The Body of God.* Minneapolis: Fortress, 1993.

McGrath, Alister E. *Christian Theology.* Cambridge: Basil Blackwell, 1994.

Meyendorf, John. *The Orthodox Church.* Translated by John Chapin. New York: Pantheon, 1968.

Moltmann, Jürgen. *The Trinity and the Kingdom.* Translated by Margaret Kohl. San Francisco: Harper and Row, 1981.

_____. *The Spirit of Life: A Universal Affirmation.* Translated by Margaret Kohl. Minneapolis: Fortress, 1992.

_____. *The Coming of God: Christian Eschatology.* Translated by Margaret Kohl. Minneapolis: Fortress, 1996.

The New Oxford Annotated Bible with the Apocrypha. New York: Oxford University Press, 1977.

Norris, Richard A. *The Christological Controversy.* Sources of Early Christian Thought, ed. William Rusch. Philadelphia: Fortress, 1984.

Pelikan, Jaroslav. *The Christian Tradition.* Vol. 1. *The Emergence of the Catholic Tradition.* Chicago: University of Chicago Press, 1971.

Pittenger, W. Norman. *The Divine Triunity.* Philadelphia: U.C.C. Press, 1977.

Prestige, G. L. *Fathers and Heretics.* London: S.P.C.K., 1979.

_____. *God in Patristic Thought.* London: S.P.C.K., 1952.

Richardson, Cyril. *The Doctrine of the Trinity.* Nashville: Abingdon, 1967.

Rusch, William. *The Trinitarian Controversy.* Sources of Early Christian Thought, ed. William Rusch. Philadelphia: Fortress, 1983.

Schlink, Edmund. *Theology of the Lutheran Confessions.* Translated by Koehneke and Bouman. Philadelphia: Fortress, 1961.

Schmemann, Alexander. *The Historical Road of Eastern Orthodoxy.* New York: St. Vladimir's Seminary Press, 1963.

Select Library of the Nicene and Post-Nicene Fathers of the Christian Church [NPNF]. 2 series. 28 vols. Edited by Philip Schaff et al. New York: Christian Literature, 1887–1894; repr. Grand Rapids: Eerdmans, 1971–1980.

Timniadis, Emilianos. *The Nicene Creed: Our Common Faith.* Philadelphia: Fortress, 1983.

Van Dusen, Henry P. *Spirit, Son and Father.* New York: Charles Scribner's Sons, 1958.

Volz, Carl A. *Faith and Practice in the Early Church.* Minneapolis: Augsburg, 1983.

Ware, Timothy. *The Orthodox Church.* New York: Penguin Books, 1963.

Whitehead, Alfred North. *Process and Reality.* New York: The Free Press, 1978.

Young, Frances. *From Nicaea to Chalcedon.* London: S.C.M., 1983.

Index